RETROSPECTOSCOPE

New and Selected Poems

Richard A. Bernstein

ONION
RIVER

PRESS

Burlington, Vermont

Onion River Press
Burlington, VT 05401
info@onionriverpress.com
www.onionriverpress.com

ISBN: 978-1-957184-85-2

Library of Congress Control Number: 2024922429

for Elizabeth,
Jessica, Chanon, Nicholas, David

"Life can only be understood backwards, but it must be lived forwards." —Søren Kierkegaard

Dear Reader,

The painter Edgar Degas complained to the poet Stéphane Mallarmé that he had so many ideas but could not complete the sonnet on which he had been laboring. Mallarmé chided his friend, telling him that poems are written with words, not ideas.

The words in this volume are mine. I have spent a long time collecting some of them. Others are more recent finds. An image I have in mind is that I, like a stationmaster of old, am tapping them out on a telegraph key, forwarding them to the next station, for you to read as you please.

This is not a high-speed operation. The key sticks. Some of the wires are down. The meaning of the words when they reach you may not be the same as I thought they were when I sent them. You'll get the idea. And, hopefully, some of the poems.

R.B.

TABLE OF CONTENTS

NINE

TEN

POSTSCRIPT

ONE

Sea Wolves

I would gladly gnaw through my ankle
to escape your sanguinity about socks
which—unlike the wolves you so admire—
do not mate for life but come apart
despite electric forces in the clothes dryer,
where I now forage on the edge of divorce.

Frantic as when a batten tore out of our jib
beating into a nor'easter, no honeymoon,
except that it was ours.

You could not fathom why I made circles
and blamed you for not watching more closely
to spot something narrow as a yardstick in an edgewise
ocean—
a measure of your seaworthiness and my arrogance—

pondering still why you are running with me,
close-hauled down these years,
still howling,
when things don't all come out in the wash.

Garden Variety

The dill you harvested last fall
has re-mustered itself this spring.
Not in neat rows,
haphazardly along the edges
and in the corners of the raised beds

I built to control the wind's breath,
the digestive systems of avian propagators,
and your propensity to love
all survivors of winter's misery.

What you call volunteers, their
agronomically correct assignation,
I call weeds, deserving nothing more
than a firm yanking!

Prompting thorny debates
not about seasoning for our salad,
but the raising of our own human cultivars:

the decisions to be made
about their bedtimes, table manners,
and Sunday school attendance.
Each one adding dirt under our nails,

while casting you as permissive Persephone
who waits until their father gets home
instead of weeding them herself,
and me as punishing Hades.

Road Salt

When we are to each other
like Antarctica,

and anger
eats through our floorboards,

I drive furiously just to prove to you
rust is not dangerous,

while you scatter nails
for traction.

Photographer Saves Marriage

She unbuttoned her blouse then shot him
when nothing less startling worked,
down to one from the bottom
to stop him from being a jerk.

By telling her how she should snap him
and which face he wanted saved,
this birdie knew some distractions
for making her subject behave.

Under red light she reads the negative
afloat on a watery scrim,
his eyes fixed on her décolletage
her eyes focused on him.

The Explorer

Between your snoring and my peeing
the dog is not sleeping
any more than we.

"Adenoids," opines doctor sleep.
"Anxiety," says the vet.
"Prostate," wags doctor pee.

After half a century of jowl by cheek
I don't need a diagnosis
to discover the couch,
a world away but still in reach.

While you—with dog encircled—
drift like a continent off to sleep.

Too hot, too cold, too firm, too old,
the new latitudes offer nothing to me
but countless sheep.

I return disappointed by the exotic East
to seek the possibility of an erotic West.
I trace your shoulder, your back,
your neck, your breast.

Walking on Glass

You would be hurt if you knew what I am really thinking,
so, I pretend I'm not thinking it and say nothing.

I would be hurt if I knew what you are really thinking,
So, you act like you're not thinking it and say nothing.

 You are better at acting like you're not thinking.

I am better at thinking I'm not thinking.

This charade is as fragile as the glass we share
twice daily after brushing our teeth—
in sickness and health, with dry hands and soapy hands—

trusting it will not slip and shatter, yet knowing it will,
despite my invocation at our wedding
to pre-empt future breakage by stomping glass.

You did not stomp. Only the groom does. You are owed one.

So, I can forgive you when you act like the glass
I am now picking out of my foot fell by itself
when you were showering.

But who's counting?

Cognition as Recursive Empathy

If you are asking for my opinion,
I will give it.

But only on the condition that
you want to know

what I am thinking about
what you think you are thinking.

Not what I think
you are thinking.

Or, I could scrunch my eyes and
scratch my head as if—

trying to think about what you think
you are thinking—

by asking your opinion of what
I think I am thinking

about what you think you are
thinking.

Hoping I would still be thinking
about what
you think you are thinking

about what
I think I am thinking...

The Brother Who Missed Our Wedding

blamed it on two flat tires to spare us
having to explain his lone Black face
in this photo album.

On our fiftieth, as I revisit the day
by flipping windows bound in leather,
and find missing
the man who still calls me "brother,"

I wonder if I deserve
his continued kinship—

and what difference made
were his image included here
in black and white?

It All Comes Out in the Wash

Such a simple task!

Open door.
Shove in load.
Close Door.
Push Start.

Trust the water-weighted heap
to come clean.

Family wash. Family tangle.
A chore? A celebration!

The family that tumbles together
sorts together.

Says so right here on the box.
When did it become more complicated?

When did the timer's tick become
so insistent?

It happened as our sweet-smelling
endearingly faded and newly warmed shrouds

no longer needed to be folded away
for later.

TWO

A Temporary Clearing

It is possible to make big mistakes with a chainsaw,
even before the cord is yanked.

Desire, deafening and stoppable only by memory—
like a tree falling wrong—
might give pause:

considering the availability of chainsaws
and the attractiveness of mistakes.

Kindling

First, build a cabin in the woods
from the woods.

Stack cut-offs underneath
for when the empty wood box

shines cold as the moon
in February.

Layer up: thermal, wool,
double gloves.

Burrow down
to maple, ash, and beech.

Split the re-cut loaves.
Count fingers.

Fill box to over-full.
Spend like a miser

then,
build a cabin in the woods.

Dream House

Attic to be allegorical,
cellar metaphorical.
Master bathroom acrobatic,
bathroom fully democratic.

Dining room for food and talk.
Kitchen table stout enough
for kneading bread
and giving birth.

Book room free of any sound,
save for Bach if he's around.
Stove that glows with phoenix wood.
Workshop hums exactitude.

Entry needs no mop or broom:
cleans itself, a fine mudroom.
Porch inhales the lilac's dew,
the front door lets my coffin through.

4' x 4' x 8'

You must think it grows on trees
that all you need to say is please,
then bucked and quartered it arrives
ready to be stacked by size.

Just like the laundry I believed
washed itself,
within a home that never needed
to be cleaned.

My job was spinning the earth,
yours was merely giving birth—
feeding and burping,
weaning and herding.

I'm not saying you should pay:
for gas
for oil
for chains
for chaps
for helmet
for goggles
and all the crap I need to tame a tree.

Or, that you should charge
for lying with me,
when other fraus would seek escape
in "not tonight" or "my head aches."

Yet, the saws
the axes
the wedges
the come along,
that could widow you for a song,

the ticks
the sweat

the cold
the scrapes
the hang-ups and close escapes

all make me want to knock on wood
and shake you into gratitude,
for cords that go for three C-notes
and get me out from under foot,

so you can keep a closer eye
on less important events:
anniversaries, births, accidents—
even death—
if it should happen by.

House Guest

After you leave
I remake the spare bed
you barely slept in.

After you leave
I want to bottle the air
you breathed.

After you leave
my mind mops
with a headless stick.

After you leave
the walls don't meet.

The Good Hurricane

When she finally arrived, after days of watching her eye
turn first away then toward us, like a bear at a picnic,

we stopped assuring ourselves there was nothing left to do
but hunker down, then did the opposite:

buckled on sou'westers and walked slantwise
to watch the lake explode.

It was in this frame of mind we first considered
she might be a good hurricane—

not like '38, that turned houses into boats,
or '54, boats into houses rocking frantically in the spindrift—

a good hurricane that prunes without uprooting, sets free
the tourists, and hastens swarms of linemen

to climb nimbly among startled birds to reconnect us
to our scrubbed and freshly admonished selves.

Pentimento

I don't own these trees
any more than I own the earth
from which they grow.

Yet, according to my tax bill,
they are mine.

A slippery bargain
allowing me to profit from stumpage
in the name of creating understory,

by releasing crowns
as prescribed by my forester
who does not stay
to bandage the skidder wounds,

or console me as I stumble
over newly gored ground
with a rainbow of spray cans
to mark new trails,

pretending I can just touch up the canvas
and not miss what is missing.

Half-Past Mud Time

Out to plant on an iffy day
I ask the straw man what he'd say
the chances this early May
of killing wind or snow that stays.

Neither more congenial to poking stalk
than chiseled beak or raking claw
of crows I put him there to scare
last fall.

I drape around his neck my coat,
and bend to give the earth a poke—
just for chuckles, not with hope—
more a query than a joke.

First, he shakes the sleeves about
then, as if he had a doubt,
turns the pockets inside out.
What to make of these eldritch signs?

After all, the coat is mine
or was, until re-assigned.
Vernal mischief,
I might opine:

a conspiracy of air and cloth
but in mud time
just enough to sorely test
a planter's troth.

Constant Maintenance

Write this down, you'll need to know it
when my nose is no longer around
for me to blow it,
mind your business or sniff the roses.

This wrench with moving jaws is not, my pet,
what you call "pliers".
The snips are for cutting tin,
the square-tipped ones for stripping wire.

The Stillson won't mark pipes.
Monkey has the teeth.
Vise-jaw has the bite.

This hammer is for banging metal,
this one for pulling nails.
You'll need a wedge beneath the claw,
when simple leverage fails.

Always tighten clockwise,
except for reverse thread.
Don't over-tighten nuts and bolts,
use a lock washer instead.

The ripsaw is for ripping,
the crosscut for crossing grain.
Rabbets don't jump out of hats,
but may be shaped by plane.

Drill bits can be sharpened,
not just thrown away.
China bristle cuts a cleaner line
than a foam brush any day.

Fifty to one is the ratio of gas to oil
in all two-cycle machines,
chainsaw, mower, trimmer blower

take premium gasoline.

Cut next year's wood this summer.
Clean both chimneys in July.
Check the static level in the well.
Call the furnace guy.

You'll get the hang of it, my love.
But unlike the Deacon's one-hoss shay,
if you don't perform some of these tasks,
this place won't last one day.

Hold your grieving is all I ask.
Check my pulse before weeping.
Don't hurry to call 911,
I might just be sleeping.

Raking Snow from the Solar Panels

After a night of heavy snow and
dreamy arguments with my father
as he chased me from room to room
switching off lights, "saving electricity,"

I clamp headphones over my wool cap,
click together aluminum tubes,
extend the blade as far as I can reach,
and pull down a white cascade thigh deep.

My stealing kilowatt hours from the sun
might have appealed to his frugality,
while challenging my audacity,
as if I were Prometheus and he were Zeus:

secretly proud of my thievery,
but warning me
not to get bigger than my boots.

THREE

Musical Prodigy

Her gift was knowing what each of us wanted
before we did.

She didn't learn that in pedagogy or psychology
class.

Un-erased from my memory board
she still stretches

from her swivel chair for the top shelf
of the supply closet

where two triangles, wrist bells, four tambourines,
a pair of cymbals, and a wood block

didn't add up to the wanton desires
of a dozen first-grade boys.

So, she asked only me to hold her chair:
very, very, carefully to keep it from spinning.

Lost Time Found

In a room with Venetian blinds,
our mother read us *Madeline*.
I have no memory of that time,
a photo prompts remembered rhymes.

Sister in pinafore and braids,
me in playsuit carefully staged
on either side of mom with book
captured for that Kodak look.

What to make of this precious scene?
Neither remembered nor a dream
yet clearly seen in black and white.

Climbing by it on the stairs I wonder
was I there? Or channeling Miss Clavel
declare "something is not right!"

Perhaps as crumbs on Marcel's tongue
summoned Combray to his brain,
my taste for synesthetic fun
wakens *Madeline* not madeleine.

Elm

Suburban legend held the elm,
first shading then dropping itself
in beetle-ravaged pieces
on my boyhood home,
was the county's second largest.

Leading inevitably to the whereabouts
of the largest: a question my mother
dismissed as irrelevant, lest she be found
to admit in her haste to flee the city for suburbia,
she had selected the wrong tree
under which to raise her children—
and the eyebrows of her neighbors—
with her city ways.

Meaning, she would not accept second best
on their behalf.

This posture put her nakedly in opposition
to a principal, a music teacher,
a priest, the road commissioner,
the director of recreation, superintendent
of schools (whose daughter was
my seventh-grade girlfriend),
and the football coach:

all men on whom I wished she would not have sprayed
the pesticide she thought was needed
to stop the infestation of anti-Semitism

I was trying to deny
by pretending I was not an elm,
while fighting my own beetles
in a county of oak and tall boys.

Coconut

(circa 1947)

Back from a trip without the children
our father presented us with a consolation prize.

Rattling with juice and meat "sweet as candy,"
he tried to crack it even before

our mother could start to unpack the leather valises
sporting new travel stickers like merit badges

earned for enduring a bumpy flight, she complained,
and a no-star hotel three blocks from the beach.

Our father—not a patient man—chose a hatchet
to attack the offering and slashed his thumb,

killing our interest in the now-bloody sphere
costing him stitches and us tears.

I bounced it in the street and bombed it
to no avail with a cinder block I called a grenade

until my uncle stabbed it open with the bayonet
he lifted from a nazi's grave.

Menorah

Five old men, their clay faces pinched
with thirty-five hundred years of worry,
raise arms awaiting candles.

Except for one. He raises a single arm.
Maybe he's tired, or had a stroke?
These things happen.

One day you can hold up both arms,
Then bam! The next day you can't.
You make do.

You get together with friends: four—
not all as strong as they used to be—
strong enough

to hold a lighted taper
in each hand above their heads
for eight days in a row.

You, with your one good arm,
will hold a candle too. Maybe,
with less to lift, you will raise yours higher.

It doesn't matter how much.
This isn't a competition. We're not interested
here in making another Statue of Liberty.

Although, that's not such a bad idea
given what our grandfathers, the "wretched refuse,"
had to endure just to meet her.

With no guarantee of admission,
their faces were pinched too,
bearing the weight of their histories.
Each of them hoping to kindle their own flame

in a new safe place—not always safer
than the old place—
but holding promise. Much as the five clay men
with nine good arms hold promise,
renewed yearly,
to increase the circle of light
against surrounding uncertainty.

The Wager

He bet his father was going to fry
at Sing Sing on Saturday.
He waved a wad of cash around.
Did anyone want to play?

I thought it was twelve-year-old
braggadocio: I, a junior counsellor
barely older than him.
What did I know?

The tent flaps whipped untethered.
The lantern wouldn't light.
We flipped mattresses, mopped the deck,
but couldn't get it dry.

Don't think too hard he laughed,
they'll do it either way.
It's just a game with them,
like sending me away.

Eleven o'clock came and went,
he had to use the john.
Eleven fifteen, not back yet.
I knew that he was gone.

Boss Man

(circa 1960)

He was my first Negro.
I was not his first Jew.
He was the boss.
I was the kid who thought he knew everything,
but did nothing to prove
I could do what I was supposed to do.

It was not that tough except I kept screwing up,
hoping to break his stony look, smile me the golden tooth
he saved for the rest of the crew
while passing the hooch from the back of his Olds
at quitting time.

I thought I could outshine them by lifting another load
as they swigged and goaded the brown-nosing Jew.

He said nothing for a week or two,
then took me aside when work was through,
unscrewed the bottle offered me some—

my face still burns
now sixty years gone.

Sandlot Legacy

You left before your moldy five-fingered glove
became a collectible for your unborn grandsons.

For me, it was still the missing face in the stands
 I kept checking for approval that was not catchable,

or the greatness I imagined erupting when I
reeled in the next flyball.

Digging under the eaves they unbury you,
count leather digits with hilarity,

pound concavity into ochre flatness.
Unselfconsciously aping their Ruths and Cobbs,

you are incarnated chromosomally
among giants.

Odysseus in the Weight Room

Jimmy's mother had no truck
with the PTA
piano lessons
the Encyclopedia Britannica
bridge clubs
slipcovers
or food that did not come in cans.

Jimmy's mother did not dress in anything but
jeans our mothers said were
too tight
tops they said were
too loose
hair they said was
too big
a housecoat they said
was so short that...

Yanked from the South
like a tooth on a string,
she never re-rooted in the North,
unlike her husband, the Colonel,
who focused on military strategy
while losing sight of the civilians:

men who
delivered the mail
put milk in the box
left parcels between the doors
sharpened knives and scissors
mowed the lawn
and stayed for coffee,
usually enhanced with something stronger.

Leading Jimmy's mother toward unsteadiness

which she treated
by positioning herself on the cellar steps
inhaling Camels
and overseeing Jimmy's crew
as we took turns lashing ourselves
to his weight-lifting bench,
straining to heave skyward
more iron than our young bodies could handle
trying to resist the siren call of Jimmy's mother.

FOUR

Owl as Oboe

—amateur poets borrow; mature poets steal. T.S. Elliot

It was neither a crow
nor a hemlock tree
but an owl on a bough
who noticed me,

and hooted his "A"
in the untuned wood
inviting my play
in his neighborhood.

Program Notes

Your *sotto voce* throat clearing on my left tells me to stop
rustling pages and just listen!

I pretend to ignore the printed words on my lap:

Gabriel Faure—Piano Quartet No.1 in C minor Op.15
composed after his fiancée's goodbye that likely...

but cannot resist discovering more:

the violinist shares a pitbull rescue with her partner...
the cellist's first love was not western music...
the viola is a Stradivari...

Rich content compared to the alphabetically listed donors and
institutional sponsors who:
made this concert linking Romanticism with Modernism...

possible even for yahoos like me who would gladly trade the music
for just reading the program notes.

Rock Concert with Philip Larkin

—Deprivation is for me what daffodils were for Wordsworth. Philip Larkin

A pause between the drenching rains
brings the warm-up band on stage.
The throb once lit will start to blaze
and keep the mob from straying.

Except to reload on pricey brew
or piss it out they stand in queues
with sudden intimates they never knew
the last time this band blew through.

Was it seventy-one or seventy-two?
Scenes of Woodstock in review
a tee shirt brags it paid its dues,
a battered hat has creds too.

"Childishness," opines the poet man
double wrapped in oilskin
to no one from his folding chair
"they think they want it back again."

A toddler naked as a jay, its parents
prancing as if they didn't have a kid
or own the sopping dog,
both trying to lick the dour bard

not feigning sleep but thinking hard
how to pen what now he understood
has been missing from his own backyard:
puppies and a childhood.

Provenance

Used to be mostly tourists
smiling and clicking, clicking and smiling.

Now it is everyone, as if the unpictured moment
has not happened

until you look at my phone
or I look at yours to see ourselves there

while still here. Though not until we see ourselves
there, are we sure.

Is this the uncertainty principle at work;
the moment that cannot be both lived and known?

I marvel at the patience of Seurat waiting two years
for seven umbrellas, two dogs and a monkey,

people on land and people afloat,
to assemble themselves on the *Île de la Jatte*

and freeze while he connected the dots
between there and then with here and now.

Canto on a Drawing by da Vinci

Hang it all, Leonardo,
there can be but one Vitruvian man!
Not the two you have tricked my eye into seeing,
while not seeing,

that you have changed the center of the universe
by raising his belly button to make his limbs touch
both the circle and the square simultaneously.

A sleight of hand—or foot—perhaps, but not
a squaring of the circle nor, *mutatis mutandis*,
a circling of the square.

Not more than I have concealed my mistakes
in the bookshelves I cobbled together for
the seven old ladies on the library committee

whose praise for my craftsmanship would cease,
if they knew how badly I botched the job
as my Skilsaw wandered offline

causing expensive oak laminate to fray,
while the eccentric wobble of my countersink bit
made holes that eccentric bungs could not plug.

It's only for children's books, I tell my prideful self,
and children are too short to feel the top edge
where the trim is a sixteenth inch proud,

or see the grain I raised sanding in the wrong direction.
Thanks to the genius of tall books, and the taller tales,
like the ones I will tell my grandchildren,

about the man imprisoned by geometry
with four arms, four legs, and—
most giggle making—two penises.

"Forever" Stamps, Really?

We trusted the glue on the back of Ike's head,
just as we trusted the tips of our tongues,
to moisten the sickle-sharp flaps
that sealed our envelopes.

We had confidence in the "Made-in-America"
thud of the corner letter box,
promising timely delivery by the cheery postman
with his special keys.

Our hearts beat with longing
for a reply to our letters,
and with dismay for those that didn't—
like a betrayal—get answered.

It was Herodotus, the historian,
not McKim, Mead, nor White,
the architects, who
engraved in our consciousness

the original version of how we know
that neither the elements, nor gloom of night,
stayed the Persian couriers from delivering
news of Xerxes defeat in 480 B.C.

Now our postman deals from his jeep
and sorts while he is driving,
gone are the letter box and keys,
his card reminds us that Christmas is arriving.

FIVE

Serendipity

On this outcropping,
the earth's skin pulled so tightly
the ribs poke through,
making sand where the sky rubs,
blueberries erupt.

Sweetness measured in millimeters
runs between our fingers
like pearls from a broken strand.

Picking not for preserves or pie but for now,
we brought only pockets and an appetite
for hiking beyond this spot that holds the sun
stubbornly against itself.

Cooling too quickly in the eroding chill,
we turn from the berryfire for someplace higher,
warmed by one last tongue-darkening handful.

Vacation Promises

Before leaving the jungle for paradise,

he promised her he wouldn't even look
at other shapely monkeys.

She promised him she wouldn't buy
bananas to bring home for everyone.

Plane delay tested their promises at the gate.

He watched football on the soundless screen,
secretly listening for the high-heeled clicks
of monkeys arriving and departing.

She sent home two bags of bananas from
the duty-free shop.

Told him they were green.

Jet Blues

I don't want to lose my place
herded to the starting gate
along with half the human race
where nothing starts except complaints.

Too late to find another flight,
a space to sleep, or catch a bite,
my red eyes scan the Delphic sign
for moving clues that might align

and point me toward a waiting plane,
that's not been cancelled or delayed,
nor assumes I'm on elastic time
grateful to be "next in line."

I am not! Neither am I entertained
by blue-tipped jets with kitschy names,
like Dream Come Blue:
no dream at all, just *déjà* blue.

Armrest with expanding seatmate
queued for take-off number eight.
Captain drawls his lullaby,
the runway calls but no birds fly.

Talking Bus Blues

Buses are valises
tied with sash cord
leaking breadcrumbs.

Buses are hamlets
strumming the eye
'til the tires stop.

Buses are filled
with stains and thighs
always empty.

Buses are coming
just leaving
never here.

Buses are you and me
hopeful as windows
headed no place.

Unclaimed Baggage

On the endless rubber conveyer
serving up planeloads for the grabbing
by the child for whom it is too heavy,
and the lady who just points,
comes your valise:
stiffly upright
among yawning duffels and sleek backpacks.

Beneath the knackered handle
your initials embossed in gold
faded from miles of worldwide handling
by careless ground crews,
when not coddled obsequiously
by a bellman aware of cash folded in your glove.

Rolling his brass ferry along carpeted rivers
toward a high-ceilinged suite
with long drapes and brocade coverlets,
he opens it for you to read the next chapter in a new time zone—
troubling you only to the extent of finding your bookmark—
and continuing to yet another adventure
for which you were always ready to spring.

Like you, the brass latches
holding together your valise no longer glow
in the dimmed lights of the baggage loop,
circling endlessly,
after the last taxi has pulled away.

Driver's Ed

Nothing good ever happens backing up,

> he said to them from the passenger seat
> before turning to eyeball the three behind him
> and repeating:

nothing good ever happens backing up,

> reading this time from his clipboard
> as if the words had been brought down
> from a mountain they had no desire to climb.

> They thought he knew about driving
> less than he knew about the football he also coached,
> and even less about sex to which he related everything.

> The also knew he was married but always flirting
> with the Health Ed teacher,
> yet they were not prepared for:

*it's like pulling out and finding the condom gone while you're
practicing parallel parking in the back seat,*

> stunning them into deflated silence.

CAVU
—ceiling and visibility unlimited

Riffling through the May edition of *Parachutist*,
not believing what I am seeing pictured:
freestyle, formation, wingsuit—
these acrobats choose
to hurtle toward the planet
from beyond the place
sufficient oxygen might change their mind,

lead them to step back inside
the doorless depositor from which they leap
toward what they call the freedom of epic tranquility
where nothing but the present exists.

I am swooped up, imagining I could be among them.

Uncertain as to how far out on this wing
I would allow myself to crawl,
I flop the magazine back on the pile
my barber has provided for her patrons
each of whom, like me, waits their turn to be swaddled
and soothed by her practiced attention.

Doubled for our delight in her mirror,
where it appears that we are true intimates,
she snips and chatters, chatters and snips,
until she showers me with secret scent,
hands back my glasses,
and I jump.

SIX

Going Home
—Woodcut 1980. Sabra Field

This truck asks: *How's My Driving?*
The next warns: *Wide Right Turns.*
One that passes promises: *The World on Time.*
Construction Vehicle Don't Follow,
instructs the one I'm stuck behind.

In their slipstreams I am hurried
toward a pastel sky that will not pause,
for me to pull over and applaud.

The Interstate does not bend itself
for fun, or draw darkening mountains down
for trucks and cars to zoom around.

Her road, ochre hued, curves like a scythe,
disappears before our eyes
in blue and lighter blue,
before we know it's gone.

Dots of light searchingly spaced,
leave us to reflect on what's been erased
from a strangely familiar scape:

even when we cannot stop to appreciate
how nature has painted its duplicate.

Yearly Highjack

My truck is hoisted on the wizard's rack,
for him to probe for violations.
Lit harshly on her underside,
she betrays my procrastination.

Tires smooth as baby's bottom,
muffler suspended by a rope,
the rust he peels in plate-sized flakes
is like a ransom note.

I am tying up his jack.
He is holding up my wheels.
Would a sticker paid by wink and nod
disclose we'd cut a deal?

There is one witness to this crime,
my mechanic doesn't work alone.
Miss July is primed to ditch the wall,
but must get dressed to testify.

Behind Big Yellow

The pulsing lights ahead of me,
the faces in the exit door,
a drawing held aloft for praise,
a disembodied middle finger raised.

The tailpipe farts.
The traffic moves in fits and starts,
then stops again.

Out squirts someone like a little me,
to the safety of the street,
from the belly of the beast

where names and punches
all are fine,
if kept below the window line.

The driver doesn't give a fig
who hits whom, so long as
he can strut his rig for pretty moms

in sun and rain, slide his window,
shoot a wave, then gallop away
like Big John Wayne.

Pride

January.

Backpack and hood, no thumb or sign,
turned and looked like he wanted a ride.

I tried to stop, slid twenty yards by him.
Snowing that hard.

Took his sweet time to come up to me.
Pushed the seat back for his knees.

His job to sit,
mine to drive.

Mused his truck was newer than mine,
been in the shop for some time.
A friend had abused it, bad.

Did I want a nip from the pint he had?
I declined.

He abruptly changed his mind about the ride.
Drop him here—anywhere!

July.

Backpack, hood, and sign.
Asking for something I couldn't read.
There wasn't time.

He stuck a bill through the driver's side—
Now we alright? Hey buddy, thanks for the ride.

There is No Free Lunch

except at Costco, the big box of horrors,
where genius marketers discovered
nobody moves product like grandmothers.

Posted at the intersections of every
boulevard-wide aisle in hair nets and vinyl gloves,
these intrepid lunch ladies offer tidbits

laced with buy-more-than-you-want pheromones,
invite you to sample just one (from the front row only),
then dare you to purloin a second,

without hoisting into your enormous carriage
a giant-sized something you didn't come to buy,
with an expiration date outliving your own.

You can try to game the system with a disguise—
I always bring an extra face—but these grandmothers
are not your indulgent nanas who forgive and forget.

They play by their own rules.
Each a Lucy Van Pelt, ready to snatch the ball
from Charlie Brown's foot just for kicks.

I fall for it again. My mission to get only toilet paper,
foiled by a smorgasbord of temptation
I suddenly discover I need all of
in quantities so vast I max out my Costco card.

The gross tonnage is enough to convert
my SUV into a low-rider,
If I can remember through my post-prandial haze
where I parked it.

Lunch at the State House

Before tucking the corner of his napkin
into the space made sliding the knot to his second button,
he cups his palm to study upside down,
the green frogs squatting diagonally on his blue rep tie.

My lucky one, he says. Wife hates it. Gift from a constituent.

He winks to include me in the conspiracy of men
at large round tables, leaping from one lily pad to another,
feeding on anything bigger than a soundbite.

Here is where our laws are made, unimpeded by Robert's Rules,
not in the great hall of yeas and nays,
where legislators hop on and off each other's arguments
in a frenzied amplexus—

the din of their croaks rising as the temperature rises—

trying to smother rebuttal with a sticky palaver,
and not get it on their rep ties with diagonal squatting frogs,
both their wives and their constituents hate.

Customer Service at the Country Store

What you want with that?
    He asked,
    before sending me down the aisle
    he knew I wouldn't find
    what I thought I wanted,
    while he squeezed the phone
    between his ear and shoulder,
    flipped on the gas pump,
    and drew singles from the cash drawer.

"Leaner," I said, "big beech,"
    trying to sound woodsy
    and more confident than I felt.

Can't do it with that.
Ain't beefy enough by half.

    I was ratcheting the handle of a farm jack
    that seemed plenty beefy to me,
    with a beefy price tag of one hundred and forty dollars.

Go ask Stumpy Tinker why he needs only one shoe
since he bought one of them jacks,
    he said,
    pulling my leg to make sure I kept both.

I'll stop by tomorrow after closing to give you a hand—
if you want.

State's Longest-serving Senator Decides Not to Ask for a Recount
—Burlington Free Press

He is of two minds
as he stands by the side of her bed
(her mouth agape, his bride of sixty years),
to shake
or not to shake her
from the sleep that escapes him.

Too early for the paper's thump.
He has paced all night,
waiting to read in black and white,
before believing he was beaten by one vote,
as reported on TV.

Who was it?
The guy who didn't want his sign?
The lady who had no time to listen?
The neighbor with dogs
who always returned his wave,
but wasn't brave enough to say he'd had his day—
that his was not the only voice
campaigning for the voter's choice—
and that twenty-four terms should suffice?

He will be ninety-two in May.
Not too old by his thinking,
to hold the *Dimocrats* at bay for another season,
or axe the *Guvnah* if he raises the *propety tax*,
even a smidgeon.

They had conversed,
he and the bride.
She said she could abide one more run,
if he'd stop waking her at night
to tell her he'd won
that morning's fight on the Senate floor.

But as she slipped from the voting booth,
the slide of the curtain,
the avoiding eyes,
caused him to be uncertain—
again, of two minds—
whether or not she could be true
before stealing away to the powder room.

Then home to eat, to rest, to wait.
She ate.
He paced.
She read.
He waited.

By ten the votes were fully in.
She slept as her book collapsed on her chest,
like the truth:
she had not voted for him.

The News in Villanelle
—for RPG

<u>Morning Edition</u>

"Police Shoot Mentally Ill Man After Standoff"

He was not by nature a violent man,
she told reporters on page one,
trying to make them understand

her father had never laid a hand
on anyone. How to her he was like the sun.
He was not by nature a violent man

except when his voices commanded
him to arm himself against their guns,
trying to make them understand

he meant business. Not a grandstand.
Without waiting till his rant was done—
he was not by nature a violent man—

they shot him. Which began
their justifications, too easily spun,
trying to make them understand

and admit what had been their plan
was to hold their fire and only stun.
He was not by nature a violent man,
trying to make them understand.

Evening Edition

"Chief Says We Had No Choice"

The chief, even in his Kevlar vest,
knows he is not bullet proof.
Riddled by the daily press,

pilloried for his apparent disrespect,
for those whose private truths
they say he doesn't try to "get,"

or make an effort to connect.
Told his men the time to move—
riddled by the daily press—

was *now* if they hoped to attest
their shots were not because they hewed
to their chief, even in his Kevlar vest,

more than public good, but to put to rest
the panic in the neighborhood.
Riddled by the daily press,

he sits alone behind his desk.
His own grief misunderstood,
the chief even in his Kevlar vest,
riddled by the daily press.

Elegy in a Country Schoolyard

—Marlboro College to close. AP November 6, 2019

The merinos have returned to rut and graze
on upland fields,
whose more recent days
saw shaggy students and their dates
turn Ultimate Frisbee into leaping foreplay.

Here, I came for Casals and Serkin.
Now, I must use my imagination
to be held again in wonderous thrall,
by unheard music
from a shuttered hall.

I cringe to think of volumes flown
unstamped from shrunken stacks,
without a borrower's address, or phone,
to ever bring them back.

The biggest loss for those displaced—
turned out of the park so to speak—
is not just the loss of created space,
but the messiness of the liberal arts,
compared with the messiness of sheep.

August in the Kingdom

We flocked to the Fairbanks Planetarium,
like the public radio sheep we have become,
to help break a Guinness World Record.

When the smoke from the food trucks cleared,
and the heavens darkened,
we guessed there were more than enough "oohs" and "aahs"
witnessing the mediocre Perseid meteor shower
than the Stout-man needed
to affirm the crowd's numerary significance,
if not our celestial insignificance.

We left early,
hoping to find an open creemee window
to satisfy our earthly desires.

Venus hung in the west like a lantern.
There were more fireflies
than shooting stars.

Until we hit Joe's Pond Country Store in West Danville,
not one open creemee window
in the whole milky way.

The man at the counter said he had just
shut down the creemee machine for the night.
Would we like, instead, to buy a ticket
to guess when the ice on the pond
would go out next spring?
They were on sale:
twenty percent off until December.

SEVEN

Word Shaping

In a catalog, I admire a low-angle plane
forged from manganese bronze
in Warren, Maine.

I can feel its heft and see
a perfect ribbon
curling out behind the blade.

I don't need another low-angle plane;
one was useful shaping
my never-finished sailboat frames.

I don't need another low-angle plane!

The boat was Joel White's take on the
classic H, first designed by Captain Nate,
seventh son in the Herreshoff line.

Twelve-and-a-half feet at the waterline
every inch of her sublime but more
work than I had time.

Joel's dad, Elwyn, called E.B,
shaped words for readers at *The New Yorker*
at home in Maine on his Smith Corona.

Invented a girl who loved a pig,
a rat-like boy just two inches tall,
and an arachnid who entrances

all she captures in her web. He edited
Will Strunk's *parvum opus*—
seventy pages last I counted—
added "style" to his mentor's plea:
use one word instead of three,
preferably a noun or verb,
adverbs sparingly.

Spathiphylum

—for A.D.

Did you really give Budd Schulberg a C+
on a story he got published in *Esquire*
just to prove you could?

Or was that my C+ on a paper
I wrote about you,
to reprove you for repeating yourself?

Nobody was meant to fly in English 2.
Like flak, your marginal lead
deflated our airships.

You wanted us to almost die in the trenches,
as you had,
before we tried to hawk our ink.

I think of you now
as I water my peace lily.
You would have called it that.

According to your book,
life and good writing
demand straightforwardness.

What would you have scribbled
had I written
this spear would turn Priapus green,

Or this scent leave birds dangling?

Valedictory Granting Metaphorical Rights to Graduates at What Was Once an All-male College

President Donne,
members of the faculty,
parents, friends, and classmates,
welcome.

Some of you may be already confused by the title of my address.
This is intentional.
Yes, English majors, it does play on the title of a poem
by our president's namesake,
but this is only one point of the compass.
The other is the use of metaphor as a life skill—
the literal title.

"Then call it that," Professor Strunk commands in *The Elements of Style*,
"Rule 18: Use figures of speech sparingly."

And, by using 'metaphorical' as an adjective,
he might have added,
You mislead your readers into thinking
the rights themselves are the vehicle
rather than the tenor of the metaphor.
Or others may think
that you are a misplaced modifier,
if they think at all—
completely another concern.

John Milton introduced us to personification in English I.
Caps off to Professor Schultz
for allowing us to consider
the life of a blind poet and the use of a dead metaphor.

Also, for having a daughter who,
by merely walking through our classroom,
stirred lustful hope into pathetic fallacy
(literally pathetic, as opposed to filled with pathos, setting aside
phallacy)*

by having us believe she would even consider a freshman's offer
with so many swashbuckling upperclassmen knocking on her door,
if not already inside.

Let me "Be clear" (*Strunk, ibid.* Rule 16), as we prepare to flip
our tassels.
Commencement, from the thirteenth century old French
commencier,
means "to start,"
along with the more common secondary usage of "graduation,"
which we have done since sixth grade
and now, perhaps for the ultimate time,
from this dear institution.
Our *Alma Mater*, having placed on us her imprimatur,
signifying we have, at least,
dipped a toe in the Pierian Spring,
whilst drinking more deeply of the holiday bowl
(like** we needed an excuse),
deserves in return that we employ in our daily intercourse
sufficient figurative language
so that she will always be "to be blest."

Brothers, let us split infinitives,
but not ranks,
in her honor.
Screw our courage to the sticking place.
Foreswear Google.
Cleave (first meaning) to the OED.
And, when we come to the fork in the road,
take it.

*Would that be a pun or a neologism?
**"Like" used here as an informal adverb,
not, obviously, as a simile.*

84

Fore!

"So much depends on the grip,"
    said the golf pro moving the doctor's
    overlapping thumbs a quarter inch
    counterclockwise.

"You look too young to be quoting him,"
    said the doctor.

"Who?"
    asked the pro.

"Hogan, the 'Wee Ice Mon,'"
    said the doctor.

"They really called him that?"

"Not to his face, in the sports columns.
But I was thinking when you said 'so much depends
on the grip,' of the line 'so much depends
upon a red wheelbarrow.'"

"I don't get it,"
    said the pro.

"It's from a poem by Williams,"
    said the doctor.

"Ted?"

"Bill. He was a doctor too. Lived in New Jersey."

"Yeah? I'm from Jersey," said the pro. "What Town?"

"Patterson," The doctor's drive slices wildly to the right.
Glass shatters.

The Poet's Handicap

I don't envy him. Driven by need
to pretend he's working,

tells his partners he's tending a poem,
that won't stop hurting.

They are free to stalk each hole,
pull the pin and then explode

as if they had aced a Pulitzer
or discovered gold.

He must draw the shade on all distractions—
a trip to the fridge, a roll in the hay—

lash himself to his swiveling chair
or open a vein.

Next, sweep his mind of last night's dew,
invite the dawdling muse to hurry up,

and play on through.

A Poet's Indemnity Policy

I would like insurance for when the words don't come.

On those days
Beatrice walked out on Dante.
Milton got lost in *medias res.*
Blake saw his dead brother.
Whitman discovered he was small.
Dickenson hid in her closet.
Yeats' falcon was blind.
Eliot ate the peach.
Williams settled for a prune.
Frost took the road most travelled.

Not a comprehensive policy:
few instructions, no exceptions, or qualifiers.
I would use it only...

In Praise of Alice

—*Everybody has won, and all must have prizes. Lewis Carroll*

"That is not said right,"
the caterpillar scolded Alice between puffs on his hookah,
after she had recited her nonsense version
of *You are Old, Father William.*

Much as Professor Donaldson
dismissed between sucks on his meerschaum,
my bastardized recitation
of the prologue to *The Canterbury Tales*
during my own foredoomed pilgrimage
to his smokey office.

Seeking redemption from the "D"
he awarded for my first try in class,
he begrudgingly changed it to a "C-"
on my second try.

That cagey old pedagogue,
deliberately withholding from my ears the ubiquitously awarded
"good job"

heard nowadays from indulgent parents
seeking favor from their indulged offspring,
whose precious gift to the world
is agreeing to observe, for now, the laws of gravity.

Bawdily Function

The movie was long, steamy, and unresolved,
until the last frame released the heroine
from her dilemma. and us to the restroom,

where there is little rest,
and much overly cordial jockeying
without eye contact.

Eavesdropping on the effortless splashes
from the urinals on either side,
I am aware anew of how age
has thrown a monkey wrench
into my plumbing.

But not my desire to compete,
by asking if anyone knew that Derbforgaill,
from the Ulster cycle of Irish mythology,
was killed by the jealous women of Uliad
for peeing the deepest hole in a pillar of snow.

Anyone did not.
Leaving me pridefully endowed
with the knowledge that if I cannot beat
these young stallions hydrodynamically,
I can still dampen circles around them
with my erudition.

Emeritus

Tucked away in the library stacks,
pretending I might yet be able to contribute
something to something,

momentarily comforted
by thinking even if I do not produce a thought,
production is still a possibility—

akin, I admit with chagrin,
to an erstwhile morning ritual
easily accomplished with coffee,
now requiring a stronger cathartic—

I hear approaching my carrell
(not using their library voices until they see me,
then modulating to a respectful hush after passing),
two former students.

"Wasn't that Doctor what's-his-name?"
   "Yeah. I think it was."
"I had him first year for Human Behavior."
   "He was a good shit."
Not exactly wording I would want the Dean
to read on my Green Sheet.
But in the moment,
despite the demotion to past tense,
a welcome and motivating re-call to active duty.

Re-union

—for the class of 1965

Fêted brethren, it is our time.

This will not be easy.
This coming back is no picnic.
My dog sense tells me it will take too much sniffing
to know again—not break for the trees and chase the fox—
as we have for twenty-five years.

We must regroup.
Why?
Should we come together
only because it is time to reassemble pieces of a shared past,
into a more-or-less recognizable present,
as a hedge against the unknowable ahead?

Is that the net?

Let me tell you something:
I was not there.
A stand-in, a doppelgänger,
wore the symbols of this place on his front and back
so immodestly,
I slipped out the middle and missed it.

I cannot have it again.
We cannot have it again.
What remains is derivative:
who we are for having been there.
And, if we are lucky, who the next might be,
for our having been.

The windows and brick of this place
still melt me.
The possibility of having anew so much to learn
is so dumbfoundedly hopeful,
I could weep.

Yet—I am reluctant to say this to you who still throw the ball
so heartily as if nothing has changed—
I do not yet know if I can count myself among you.
It is not a matter of choice alone.
History written only by winners has not guts.
Worse, no soul.
What have the dead to report?
Who of the living among us is already dead?
Answers are not expected.
A tugging for understanding is.
If, at the laying up of the next homecoming bonfire,
you find your shoulder against mine,
our hands locked in lifting,
you will then know I have felt the tug
and have come along.

EIGHT

Pre-med

The possibility of my getting the older brother I had always wanted,
dropped to zero when I became eleven.

Not because I found my mother's diaphragm hidden in her
laundry bag. Or my father's condoms stashed with his cufflinks—

both useful erotic secrets I could swap with my friend, Donald,
for a peak at his parents' top-shelf copy of the *Kama Sutra*—

but because a thing called "fibroid" had taken the place off where
a brother would be. If my mother wanted one. She did not.

Instead, I got to see her incision, smiling greatly, itchy,
and immodestly displayed to everyone, including me,

lest I needed reminding of the price she had paid
for my privilege of birth during the worst blizzard on record,

alone in the delivery room with a nasty nun for a nurse,
and "your father in the bar getting drunk with my doctor."

Kindling all my rescue fantasies, this scenario left me no choice
than to begin the long slog toward becoming for my patients

the older brother they might also have wanted in their times of need—
except for those who wanted an older sister.

Medici, Cura te Ipsum

—Physician, Heal Thyself

I stuck a blade into my cadaver's eye,
to see what was inside.

I stopped a dog's heart ten times.
Restarted it nine.

The hand I tucked between a stranger's thighs,
bailed blood all night. I would not cry.

Hooded and in sanguine robe, I pledged
an oath that would be my guide.

As a house officer, I believed I could fly.
Years of practice proved that a lie.

Now, I lift the bandage from my eyes,
soaked with the doubt I have denied.

Passing, A Bedside Lesson

Paged to Blue Surgery bed 719,
I knew we would find
the detritus of well-intentioned futility
delivered by the crash cart littering the bed.

I heard silence from the chest.
Turned my wrist to note the time.
She cupped his other hand in hers.

Staring into his unblinking eyes,
without opening her ribboned black book
she introduced herself to him,

a courtesy that I had overlooked.

As a Psychiatrist You...

Yes?
As a psychiatrist you must—
Yes—
As a psychiatrist you must know—
Yeas—
Or maybe you have heard—
Mmm—
I know someone who—
Uh huh—
I don't know how to say this the right way.
Use your mouth.
That's funny! I didn't think psychiatrists were supposed to be—
Funny?
Yeah. Funny. You know, funny, like ha ha, not like the other kind.
(He makes a circle around his ear with his forefinger).
Well, some of us are funny.
Really? You mean a little—(he repeats the gesture)—
Cuckoo?
I'm glad you said it. I could never say that to you. Not to your
face anyway.
But you might think it?
Don't get me wrong. I would never say it.
You're not like that.
What do you mean?
Someone who would say something unpleasant to another person.
Well, I can get angry if that's what you're asking.
And then you might say something unpleasant?
Yes, I guess—
You're not sure.
I'm sure.
You don't sound sure.
Well, I am! How do I sound now?
How do you think you sound?
I think I sound—Hey, what are you doing?

100

I'm talking with you.
No, you're not! You're just playing psychiatrist with me.
And the difference is?
You know damn well what the difference is.
You're beginning to sound a little angry.
Don't tell me how I'm feeling.
I'm telling you how you're sounding.
You, (buzzing his lips dismissively), would like that, wouldn't you? Getting your kicks making me angry while you do nothing.
That's not how I get my kicks.
How do you? I bet you won't tell me.
I pick my nose.
What!
Just the left side. I'm left-handed.
You have got to be joking.
I wouldn't joke about something like that.
I don't believe you. You're just saying that as part of your technique to get me—to make me think you have hang-ups too.
I can't make you do anything.
Aren't you supposed to get your problems fixed before you try to fix mine? I mean isn't that how you got your psychologist license or whatever it is you're supposed to get before you—
I'm a psychiatrist.
That's what I said.
You said psychologist, get your psychologist license.
Whatever. What's the difference anyway?
You said psychologist.
It doesn't matter what I said or what you said. I'm saying you should get your shit together before you try to help others get their shit together.
You said psychologist.
You're beginning to sound a little angry.
I get angry when people don't know what they're talking about.
And I get angry when people don't answer my questions.
So, what's your question?

On Being Greeted by a Patient Not Seen for Thirty Years

Please wait while I try to retrieve your name,
from the magic slate of your face.

Please wait while I riffle through my files,
unable to find the key to unlock it.

Forgive me for wasting the now,
searching for a then, without which
there is nothing old between us to renew.

Perhaps a new, new, that must excuse itself,
and leave me red-faced, will convince you
that despite my present spacy space,

there is a vivid you, who—
to my relief and pleasure—
gracefully takes your place.

Nearly Fatal
—for V.G

Tell me it was an amphetamine-crazed yahoo
hauling ass to the Big Apple in his eighteen-wheeler,
who downshifted through your windshield.

Tell me it was a born-again biker from East Overshoe,
flying by his ear buds to the Dead,
with no place but your front seat to park his Harley.

I will believe you.
I will believe you because you are a poet.
Even unconscious.
Even on a respirator when only your eyes speak.

The news came in pulses of ruby light and siren scream.
Did reflex shoot your arm out to the empty passenger seat?
Were you wearing clean underwear?

Healing comes in tiny pieces fit for a baby bird.
Makes you wonder if you will ever chirp again.
Let alone fly.

You will! From the depths of your plaster.
From the pain beyond needle, nightmare sharp.
From death's rehearsal that died without you.

Parkinson's
—for B.R.

We report you like the weather. Bad yesterday. Today worse.

> "Did you hear he fell off a ladder then drove himself
> to the hospital,
> gearshift stuck in first?"

They sent you home with fifty stitches.
You climbed right up again,
to show your flesh defies the twitches.

You are a very stubborn man.

Have we mistaken your intent to live as if your life were yours,
despite diminishment?

We are not as brave.

We insist on keeping in our mind's eye
the much of you,
before you were less.

Our selfish need for symmetry
denies your right to seek redress in compromise:
half man, half disease,
chimera and bellwether.

We peck you
with the mad belief
our bleats will make you better.

Dementia

When you bring up your dead, it is always tepid news.
Stories already read.
Names already excused
from the necessity of living.

You announce the missing from your circle—
no longer a ring—
for those of us still listening
to your endless recounting.

Recounting without remembering,
yet citing every slight and bruise.
The interest on each wound accruing daily,
without forgiving.
The bride's mother still stewing over "regrets" on *her* wedding list.

Once you were the center of all that came and went.
My world you invented.
Your time is what I spent,
unwisely it must now seem.

I am not blind to your struggle, nor deaf to your rage.
I understand your trouble, but will not abide
having you unravel while you are still alive.

When You Don't Know Whether to Kill Them or Kiss Them

My name is Dylan, he says,
turning his baseball cap backwards as he stands.
I broke into your houses and stole stuff.

This is my mother. (Points).
Guilty, says her half-raised hand.
And my old man. (Points again).
Not my fault, according to his crossed arms.

Thank you all for being here tonight. This ain't easy.

The rows of empty folding chairs in the cafeteria speak for
themselves.
The "all" of us who could be here—
who should be here—
are not.

Yet, where is it written that drinking bad coffee from Styrofoam
cups,
or thumbing aspirational pamphlets,
ever stopped one needle?

I haven't used since I got out. That's four months ago.
So, if you're missing something now, it ain't me.

Even Chief Hart, on the panel to my right, laughs.
His trooper hat is on the table.
The last time he saw Dylan was in the back of his patrol car.

We clap for Dylan who has turned his cap to shadow his face.
He has slumped down between his parents
as the school psychologist begins her slide presentation.

Dylan's father unfolds his large arms,
places one around Dylan's neck in a chokehold,
takes off his son's cap,
and places his lips on top of the boy's head.

Supervised Injection Sites
—a "harm-reduction" model for the treatment of opioid addiction

I swear by Apollo
that despite my best intentions,
I will not succeed
by discretely dispensing the keys to the opium den
as if they were M&Ms.

I swear I will hold my tongue,
not judge, cajole, or harangue,
as I inject myself with the belief
that swapping dirty needles for clean
is not the same as extinguishing your fire with gasoline.

Here you will get a private niche,
distilled water, alcohol swabs, and a tourniquet—
even condoms for the fun of it.
But don't be fooled, this shit ain't free.
I am not Saint Nick.

You will not be redeemed by this devilish swap.
Apollyon's, not Apollo's invention,
that will lead only to grief,
and leave you at the mercy of your demons.

Despite the best of my intentions.

House Call

The front door opens.
Here is my patient in the entry.
No knock. No bell.

He had called from a pay phone.
Disconnected before he finished.
A cab at the curb makes a U-turn.
Speeds away.

Our last contact... five years? Ten years?
At the State Hospital.
Manic. Psychotic.

His coat is wet and heavy.
Too heavy for just being wet.
He sees me eye the distended pocket.
Not a gun, he tells me,
pulling out a jar with a screw top.

He wants me to kneel and pray with him
over the ashes of his father,
dead from a stroke,
finally free of his having to kill him.

The Second Stage of Grief

—*after E. Kübler-Ross*

She drove to my office for a first visit
in a truck with a cherry picker
mounted on the back.

She kept her helmet and insulated gloves
on her lap. Said she would never lie down
on my fucking couch.

Said she hated all men, her boss more than
anyone. Loved her husband even though
he was twenty years older and in a wheelchair.

Told that because of her anger problems,
she had to see a shrink or lose her job.
That was crazy!

The only thing wrong with her were men—
her asshole co-workers especially—
who kept hitting on her.

She had a loaded pistol in her glovebox,
two Dobermans to guard her house.
One dog had the same first name as mine.

What was the other's, I asked.
Same as your last, she said,
teasing with clear blue delighted eyes.

She came to my office twice a week for five years.
She laughed. I laughed. She cried. I cried.
She quit coming when her second Doberman died.

Phone Call

You called me about your daughter.
Thinking, perhaps, that I know something about her you don't.

A curious idea given you were present at her birth,
and spent almost twenty years watching her like a hawk.

I was privileged to share only minutes of her time,
during a year of missed appointments, scheduled then cancelled.

Her diagnosis? I cannot share. The central conflict of her life?
Men: you, me, all of us (I am saying too much here).

No. She never said she wanted to kill you.
I would have had to tell you that.

I can say that I have a full understanding of,
and complete empathy for, the pain you are experiencing.

I, too, love your daughter—only professionally of course—
but I know my feeling cannot be requited nor my wound healed.

Holes

Instead of saying he killed himself,
she says suicide took him.
Even though the two exit holes in the garage roof—
not there before he pulled the trigger—
testify that he meant it.

This thought keeps slipping from her grasp,
as he did,
for most of their marriage.
The way her wedding band slips without friction
over her knuckle.

Was it always that easy to take off?
Or, has her practice of removing it in preparation,
worn it to a thinness that could not hold?

For days they have been coming to inspect the holes:
detective with chalk and ruler,
coroner with notepad and tweezers,
hazmat team in rubber suits.

Everyone except a man to fix the roof.
She started looking under "repair,"
then totally blanked on how to use her laptop.

Fleeing to the garage, she kneels on cold concrete
trying to bleed two separate tracers of sunlight
into one with Dawn and a scrub brush,
as if the truth were not written on the stone.

Blood Draw

—Blood is a very special juice. J.W. von Goethe.

You have good veins, she said.
    Thank you, I said.

I miss most doctors the first time.
    Call this the second time, I said.

What kind of doctor are you anyway?
    A retired one.

I think my sister was a patient of yours.
    I couldn't say.

Oh, right. Confidentiality. Right?
    Right.

Her name was Marybeth Francesco.
    Was?

She got married. Her last name now is—
    That's okay. Give her my best wishes.

Can I do that?
    Absolutely. And I'll need an elastic wrap. I'm on a blood
    thinner and it won't stop bleeding without one.

It doesn't say that here. It's not in your record.
    I'm saying it.

*I'll need to get permission. I just can't take your word for it
even though you're a doctor.*
    That's fine. I'll hold my arm up here for a while. I have time.

My Turn: Shivering in the Emergency Room

She promised me a warm blanket.
Said it was the best part of having to be here.
I waited, unblanketed,
thinking only of the worst part,
until the shift changed.

Her replacement asked if there was anything she could do
to make me more comfortable.

I suggested a warm blanket.
Not sarcastically,
as I figured that would not work.

Yet, with chattering teeth I was uncertain—
short of taking my pain elsewhere—
what would.

She partially covered me with a cold tarp
smelling of toasted oats.

She said it was all my insurance company would allow
because of last year's poor harvest.

I sensed the unease of other animals
on either side of me in their curtained stalls.
Heard their teeth,
Smelled their fear.

NINE

Double Take

We have two sets of twins.
(I usually have to say it twice).

We have two sets of twins,
one girl and three boys.

Identical?

Both fraternal.

What are the chances of that?

According to Hellin-Zeleny's law
One n-tuple birth per 89^{n-1}.

Wow! I never realized it was so high.

Neither did we.
Neither did we.

That Mother-beat

Your mother felt your drumming
before you were here
and drummed back.

Kneeling, with my ear to her blue belly tracks,
I heard something,
but held back from your drumming,
even after you were here.

Even as I held you—thin as a drumstick—
against myself,
you tried to drum away my deafness.

Your drumming should be my drumming, I thought.

You persisted with your own beat until—
through my feet—
I felt what your hands were driving at:
one on snare, one on high hat.

Kicking in the big drum,
my man,
my son,
got that mother-beat so bad

he can waste some on his dad.

Queen of the Boxes

You tried on apartments like earrings,
as much to be seen
as to see the look on your father's face:
the green one over the saloon
approved of as much
as the gold one in your left nostril.

Jumping out of the nest does not always fly.
Roommates sour. Landlords gouge.
Boyfriends think with their gonads.
Sometimes, even home can look good,
albeit in a limited way.

What you take with you
can burden or grace.
I recall a stuffed chickadee hopping into my backpack
vacating a rented flat sixty years ago
in Berkeley.
Caught by the owner, I shamefully relinquished
more than I was stealing.

It goes that way
when you are travelling light—
or believe you are—
when every desideratum
is a nail necessary for a soup
as filling as gruel.

Daughter, you were too good
at declaring your independence,
and then decreeing
that I could help you move.

Circumnavigation

A summer gust through the bedroom window has toppled
upon my model of Gipsy Moth IV
an adjacent framed photograph of my daughter-in-law's left
nipple—
with newborn grandson attached—
as beheld by his father's Nikon.

The one-inch-equals-one-foot scale replica
beating hard to windward across the polished top of my
bureau,
suffered injury to her dental floss stays,
and uprooting of her lifeline stanchions
fashioned from finishing nails.

No stranger to damage wrought to his craft by the Roaring Forties,
Sir Francis Chichester might have appreciated the verisimilitude
of the scene wreaked by the estivial breeze.

But what would his three-and-a-half-inch self
have made of the billboard-sized breast—
visible without his spyglass—
I espy from the leeward side of the same nuptial bed
that launched my grandson's father?

Soccer Grandpa

He's got his grandpa's shanks:
thin ankles, and hardly enough moo in the calf
to keep his socks from drooping like he does,
riding the bench.

All but invisible to the coach,
whose favorites play the whole game,
unless the lead is big enough for subs.

That number four, I say to him in the car—
now droopier because he didn't play,
and all he got was a post-game orange
proclaimed rotten—

is a real hustler:
trying to keep my praise moderate,
while picturing number four's piston legs,
streaming blonde hair, and nose for the ball.

Grandson crumples against the door.
He's a jerk. He doesn't even know if he's a boy or a girl.
Why does he get to play with us?
It's not fair...

What would make it fair? I ask,
reaching for a teaching moment on gender acceptance
without a lesson plan.

If he didn't get to call himself Charlie.
That's my name!

I Know it When I See it

—threshold test for obscenity. Potter Stewart in Jacobellis v. Ohio, 1964

How long should a grandchild stretching toward adolescence
be allowed to linger in the bathtub?

How long should a Congress well past term limits
be allowed to lather without rinsing?

Grandma and I, on edge with disbelief at the sordid news on TV,
try to disattend to the distant bubbling

from the Jacuzzi in our bathroom, where our visiting granddaughter
is discovering the pleasures of her body:

a body that will have to withstand my thinly disguised
discourse on the need for shorter baths to "save water,"

and scalding attacks she and her sisters will endure
from politicians turning dangerous spigots.

Trout

When they are too big to just eat,
Dan hangs them on his walls.

There's the fat rainbow over the bathroom sink,
within earshot of the tumbling faucet water.
Hopefully, some comfort to the glass-eyed fellow
into whose gullet I stare scrubbing my hands.

Dried, I run my fingers along his flank,
still silken under layers of shellac,
creating a haptic connection to fishing
with my sixth-grade friend beneath a stone bridge
on the Sawmill River

where he showed me
how he milked his enormous penis.

An act my father called abusing myself,
when he caught me trying unsuccessfully
to perform it in our bathtub,

after waiting what he felt was long enough
to demand *what the hell are you doing in there?*
Before pushing through the latched door,
and standing above me ready to shoot a fish in a barrel.

Light of Dogs

—*Outside of a dog a book is man's best friend. Inside of a dog it's too dark to read.*
Groucho Marx

Getting a dog is like getting religion;
They are neither our children nor our parents.

They are both, a heresy to those who eschew
anthropomorphism until they lose a dog—

which has no comparison—
as there is so much human suffering

in the remains of what remains
of their totemic lives

to illuminate and enlighten us.

Words Cannot Express

The thought of somebody rubbing my body
gives me the creeps.

Somebody doing it would be worse.
I have never had a massage.

I recall no trauma or injury to explain
my aversiveness.

I do like hugging. Less so being hugged.
What I really like is rubbing my dog.

I think she likes it too.
She tells me with her sighs,

and with her eyes that slowly close
when I reach the right spots

at the angle of her jaw
and behind her ears.

I feel her pleasure
through my own body:

first in my chest, up into
my jaw where the vice loosens,

then down my right hind leg
(if I had one),

that treadles in sync
with hers.

Back Bay Alarm Clock
—Boston, 1967

Some loose-lipped gull
tired of bickering
over the shared take
at a nearby clam stand,
breaks open his breakfast
on my fire escape,
then cries for his mate
to come and get it.

High cuisine on the half shell
rings down the iron stairwell
like a glockenspiel,
chasing the overtones of sleep
from my waking ears,
without arousing from his
feigned snooze my cat,
on his window perch,
conjecturing which bird
he will choose first to eat.

Invasives

A neighbor who swears she loves dogs to death,
calls about ours barking
when she walks hers on our trails.

Having read up on dog speak,
I know that barking has meaning
(sometimes I do it myself),

aware that if my dogs were French,
they would correct my pronunciation,
but know I was making a good faith effort
to communicate with them.

Not so my neighbor, who insists I am minimizing
the risk she is taking on her walks.

Burrowing down to the buried bone,
the *raison d'etre* for her calling me: invasives!

Did I know I had a whole field of wild parsnips,
with "sap so poisonous it can kill you?"

Henceforth, she would not be walking her dogs
on our trails, and we should take the same
precaution with our dogs on her trails
(the ones she doesn't have),

because "one might get loose."
Dogs or parsnips? I might have asked.
But didn't.

Breakfast with My Soon-to-be Ex-Daughter in Law

She called the undertaker when her father died—
something she had never done before,
for something her father had not done before—
seeking direction and comfort.

She got neither.
Instead, a terse question edged with impatience
from a voice sounding as old as her father's.

"Up or down?"

I am as puzzled as she was,
until the punchline she delivers
with uncertain laughter
between bites of English muffin.

He was trying to find out if
he would have to lug the body up,
or drag it down from her parents' apartment.

I laugh too,
unsure why she is telling me this now,
her father twenty years dead.

Outside the kitchen window
chickadees are storming the feeder.
A woodpecker forsaking the suet cage
is prospecting for insects in my cedar siding

high up near the ridge—
where a man my age shouldn't be climbing—
my anxious thoughts fly
to the future of my house
on whose intactness I had always counted.

The Morning After the Day After the 2016 Presidential Election

Nothing has changed this morning from the morning before,
when everything had changed.

Water still arrives in the faucet. The newspaper, padded with ads,
keeps losing weight.

The dogs have had breakfast. The quotidian tasks
call for what attention we can muster.

Tonight, the winners will make winning babies.
The losers' dreams will all be stillborn,

like the predictions of the toothless pundits
who assured us that what happened could not possibly happen.

You shred paper to add, along with last night's
half-eaten dinner, to the compost bin outside the kitchen.

Your bare feet make tracks in the frost-stiffened grass,
leading to slippery puddles at the sink where you rewash clean
dishes.

I didn't spin it, you confess. *There was a family of mice in the
bottom of the barrel and I thought they had been through enough for
one morning.*

TEN

Widow's Walk

The weathercock wheels on the dizzying wind.
Her barometer falls all day.

A slamming shutter
reveals not just the house,
but herself in disarray.

Up, up, she climbs.
Up from crocheting
a shroud for the howling sea.

Still higher, to the crosstrees.
Against the railing wind she leans, untethered,
trying to fix through her glass the harbor gate,

unable to wait, or not to wait,
for the cathedral-voiced buoy
to stop its tolling.

On Ferry Time

We pick our tickets in March when they are still green.
I put mine in my desk
where it can ripen until September.

I peek at it from time to time
with the pleasure of anticipation and a tinge of worry
that something might—though in forty years it hasn't—
stop the countdown's desultory creep.

Until, tying the surf rods onto the roof of the jeep,
smacking our heads in disbelief,
we still have six hours and three hundred miles
to catch a ferry that doesn't give a hoot
about anybody's schedule but her own.

Woods Hole!
Up the ramp and into the hold.
Packed like cans in a cooler, we slither out
trying not to ding the Mercedes six inches from our door.
Then climb towards sunlight,
to the windbreaking slant of the pilot house
and our meeting spot among the turtled lifeboats.

The horn startles.
The pilings march backwards.
Our feet throb.
Gulls lift and swoop.

Will I? She extends toward me an ancient Brownie Hawkeye
and demonstrates by holding it to her eye what she wants
before casting into the air
from a shopping bag crumpled between her sandals,
fistfuls of coarse grey ash
that disappear as if they never were.

The Revenge of War

He left America on two stout legs
with an open heart,
a knapsack,
a helmet,
and an M-16 he promised himself
never to use.

He came back from Bagdad
on two stout legs,
with a broken heart,
a knapsack,
and a helmet.

He got a German Shepherd puppy
he named Lieutenant Bong,
to honor the memory of his friend, Cliff.

He taught Lieutenant Bong
how to sit, stay, come,
crawl on his belly,
and salute with his right front paw.

He took a selfie with Lieutenant Bong
under the weeping willow
he planted to honor Saif,
his Iraqi driver.

Before he sent it, he remembered
dogs are *najis*, impure, in Islam,
and would contaminate the memorial
in the eyes of Sarif's family.

He sat Lieutenant Bong under the willow
and carefully explained
they must come up with a new mission
for not forgetting what had happened
in the place that was not America.

Great Silence

America piped and grandpa heard.
Through the Great Gate
and down the Cossack-cold Dnieper,
it said, "Come."

So, he did.
As oats in a troika,
as a goat to Odessa,
as a huddled mass
to the rummage sale on Ellis Island.

He swapped dreams like an overcoat.
In the steamy hold he made up
cousins near Hoboken,
a job in Canarsie,
a birthdate,
even a new name,
while the custom's pencil tapped impatiently.

He took the bridge to Brooklyn
after buying it twice.
The streets were not paved with gold.
They were not even paved.
He apprenticed himself to a magician
who ran out of rabbits.

He found America on a rental farm,
then lost it to the bank during a strike.
Milk soured in his pockets.
The melting pot melted.
The rainbow cracked.
It rained for forty days.
At night his ulcer thundered.

Brother-in-law, Morris, made it big in shirts,
and asked for a partner.

Grandpa said "no."
He had pride.
Morris made it big in suits,
and asked for an assistant.
Grandpa was "busy."
Morris opened a plant in the Garment District
and needed a manager.
Grandpa nodded, and picked from the line of sewers
she with whom he spent seven decades and
produced two children,
one of whom went off to war in '42
on whose Eastern front was the bottomless pit
called *Babi Yar* that had swallowed grandpa's parents
after he left.

Grandpa never told this to his son.

The Perfect Project
—for J.D.

You need to build something, not weep,
because you are a carpenter not a weeper.

You built a hope chest when you had no hope.
A bookcase when you had no books.
A table for six when only she and you
were left.

Now you must build her coffin,
and you are out of wood.

Grief is a perfect project:
exacting, dimensionless,
more critical of your craftsmanship
than you will ever be,
with nothing to show for the effort
except the effort itself—
which is everything.

I can, as did *Eliphaz* the Temanite with Job,
sit by your side in silence for seven days,
each alone in separate remembrance.

Or we can build something together,
as building is preferable to weeping,
and more efficient than weeping and not building.

Death by e-mail

I found two cans in the attic,
their labels long gone—
probably beans and corn—
in a nest of waxy twine.

I couldn't imagine why until
untangled, I remembered
stretching it from Jimmy's window
to mine.

The ideal distance
for vibrations to carry,
according to Mr. McBride,
who taught fifth grade science

and died before our eyes
as unexpectedly as Jimmy,
sixty years later,
from cells that metastasize,

spreading like the e-mails
old friends tap out searchingly,
for words that don't sound
like they came from a can.

A Romance in Two Dimensions

—after E.A. Abbott; Flatland: A Romance in Many Dimensions. 1884.

We screwed up every chance of knowing each other vertically.
With us, like Abbott's flatlanders, it was all horizontal.

Our ways of knowing stopped at length and width
without the benefit of height.

Imbedded as we were in the surface of things,
like the circle and the square

who could not discern the other's shape without
feeling the angles.

Decades later your obituary gives you a third dimension:
wife, mother, scientist, professor.

You are now a sphere. I am still trying to be a cube
and not fall off the edge of the earth.

Nickel to You, John
—*for J.K. 1948-2023*

It came as no surprise.
You gave us two years to join you
in denying what was right before our eyes:
you were dying.

You diagnosed yourself as "fine,"
in answer to all our queries,
and from rushing to the premature closure
that ultimately matures and closes for all of us.

You put your foot in the door,
and held it there till the ending,
allowing time for what needed to be let in, in.
What needed to be let out, out.

We called you heroic because your courage
in the face of your suffering was.
What we really meant was *menschlichkeit*,
the German translation of Cicero's *humanitas*,
signifying the best qualities of a human being.

Etymologists tell us the word migrated into English
through the Yiddish *mensch*, as a "loanword,"
assimilated from one language to another
without translation.

Reminds me a little of the Buckeye
who replanted himself in Vermont
without digging up his roots in Ohio.
Essentially on loan to us—
as each of us is to one another, date of return uncertain—
which played well to your two dispositions:
adventurer and historian.

You first led us,
then regaled us with your version

of what we just had done.
Or thought we had.

Now we are reeling you back to the poker table,
to the pile of chips awaiting your contribution.
You hover above and we,
in grateful chorus, repeat, louder,
"nickel to you, John."

Taps for the Last Trumpeter

What Joshua or bug-eyed kid
would have the brass to blow down the sun?
Or stir the air above rows of stone
with horn-sized bits of scale
connecting the bones of here and now
with the bones of not here and not now?

Open the case.
Open your heart until you know you can play it
by heart without weeping.
(Or stumbling up to the G without cracking),
that you will hold for its full-measured glory,
before letting it sigh like a campfire into coal.

Or before we are ready to unclasp,
stand in silence and wait,
for the echo that re-ignites our breath
for one last good night.

POSTSCRIPT

P.S.

"The trouble with poetry is," writes Billy Collins, "that it encourages the writing of more poetry." This truism I discovered for myself upon receiving the publisher's copy of the book you are holding, along with the conundrum of how to add some of the poems I had forgotten in a folder, without having to reformat the entire text of the volume. My solution is this postscript (which I could have called an afterword or addendum, but I found P.S. more "poetic"). I hope you will as well.

R.B.

The Trouble With Words

You have asked for my opinion.
I will give it:

Don't!

Your face fills with disappointment.
I am wishing I had no opinions about anything,

and could scratch my head to show you
I am just as confused.

That would have been my gift to you,
(not giving what you asked for
but what you wanted and could not ask for),

and my gift to me for knowing it.

We are with our words what Shaw
said about his home and ours:
two countries separated by a common language.

Simple Arithmetic

First, find the price of one apple.
Do it by dividing apples by apples
not price by apples.

I would like an apple for each time
I got it wrong. But fruit is not at
the core of my problem.

It's the line between top and bottom,
the "goes into" line that has
always confounded me.

How can three fourths mean
the same as three divided by four
when four is bigger than three

and cannot go into it
without turning three into thirty
(just for now) by putting

a period after it and adding a zero?
This would give me seven apples
and part of an apple or

seven apples plus parts of apples
depending on how I slice them.
No more exact

than a chicken and a half laying
an egg and a half...
reminding me I did have the chicken,

but no drinks and should be sober enough
to figure my share of the gratuity, without
the rest of you pretending not to watch.

Discretion

*"I say beware of all enterprises that require new clothes,
and not rather a new wearer of clothes." —Henry David Thoreau*

Used to be "a penny for your thoughts" meant
somebody wanted to know what you were thinking.

Used to be if you had something to say
you didn't put it on your tee shirt—

at least not the front— unless you wanted to see
what the eyes reading you thought of what they read,

while they are asking themselves *why anyone would
want to be seen in that?*

The same question is on your mind as you fling from
your bureau onto the bed an array of today's choices,

each of which raises the possibility of your being misread.
Inadvertently stitched by your threads

into a new self, disagreeable to your old self,
by wearing the wrong label.

Thoreau without a doubt would have you wear it
inside out.

Without My Cell Phone How Will I Know?

Our host has snapped every course as presented.
I can't wait to see how she will frame desert.

What is it about this meal that demands such documentation?
What cries out to be remembered, or not forgotten?

Visitors to the Grand Canyon, tourists at the Great Wall
may be excused. (Think Heraclitus and the river).

The mole in his burrow does not need a recording
to recreate his first hearing of the *Ode to Joy*,

nor do lovers need breadcrumbs to agree on what they were doing
when their toes first curled.

They were *there!* Are we not here *now?*
Have the gears sent the top spinning so fast all colors

have blurred to white with no undocumented reality
between the blue snuggly and the black hearse?

Olympian

Every four years we spread our blankets
to take in the worldly extraordinary.

Sometimes a star falls. Meteor becomes meteorite.
The TV makes sure we have seen it.

A voice with a microphone asks:
how do you feel?

As if it were not enough that you had made us
believe this time, this one time,

effort would best entropy, practice would
defeat gravity,

and you will have painted the heavens
with the beauty of your desire.

Help

"Can I help maybe with you," she asked,
her intention more direct than her English
while performing a graceful double
hammerlock on herself,

freeing with her fingertips the two clips
inhibiting progress toward her breasts
and my desires.

It was a question I had never been asked
in that situation. My usual high school dates
played defense,

requiring every athletic move I knew
to gain a tactile touchdown
and earn scoring points,

which counted for nothing in Stockholm
from where she came as an
exchange student senior year,

"to find out boys in the America,"
she said,
which I helped maybe
her learn a little bit about.

Deer Crossing Signs

Yellow diamonds with leaping stags,
waving antlers like eight-point flags,
warning in English underneath
some ungulates have been taught to read.

What if it was up to them,
where to cross safely
and not cause mayhem?

Highway deer would do the work—
hanging bellies, orange vests—
cursing the jerks who don't abide
and speed on by the yellow signs,

and removing their hard hats
for the glassy-eyed kind
tied to car roofs with bailing twine.

Wrong place! Shout the does
watching from windows, talking on phones.
Years as crossing guards;
mothers know.

Our conceit corrals us to believe
we know better where they should meet
to freely dare their highway leaps.

When they, for eons before our intrusion,
have trampled their instinctive byways
without peril or confusion.

"Wimoweh"

Most of what I know about getting along
I learned from Mrs. Seeger's son,
the Abraham Lincoln of folk music,
who emancipated my White suburban consciousness
more in a single song than did nine years
of Sunday school.

He gave me a hammer and told me to swing it everywhere.
No further instructions. Didn't matter if I bent the nail
or missed entirely, as long as my intentions
were to build a stronger world.

Same with the bell. Clang the hell out of it.
Wake the neighborhood—even Mrs. Willoughby
who called the cops for any noise louder than
a lawn sprinkler—shake out of their torpor
folks from Rhymney to Birmingham.

Tell them the bankers are taking it all.
The miner's children are shivering for lack of coal.
A plane load of deportees lost its wings
over Los Gatos canyon and

if nobody gives a Joe Hill about anything,
it won't be just flowers disappearing.

Pete, I believed everything you sang and
everything I sang after you put the words in my mouth.
Arlo said you sang them before us, then with us
at the same time. How did you do that?

Your spirit keeps driving the big boat up the Hudson.
The wheel, our earth, turn, turn, turns
through every season.

You, the lion who does not sleep,
still pulls on your stocking cap, spans the long reach
of your five-string, raises your chin

and sticks your neck out for all of us.

Notes

Garden Variety (p.4)

Persephone, according to Greek mythology, was the vegetation goddess. Daughter of Zeus and Demesne, she was lured by Hades, god of the underworld, into the underworld after she accepted some ripe pomegranate seeds from him.

Walking on Glass (p.8)

It is traditional at Jewish weddings for the groom to stomp on a wine glass. The usual explanation for this is to remind the couple that there will be sorrow along with their future happiness.

Raking Snow from the Solar Panels (p.26)

Prometheus stole fire from heaven and brought it to earth, angering the gods. Zeus punished him by chaining him to a rock where an eagle fed daily on his liver.

Lost Time Found (p.32)

Madeline is a children's book by Ludwig Bemelmans in which Ms. Clavel is a character. *Une madeleine* is a sweet, spongy French cookie the smell of which transported the writer, Marcel Proust, back to his home in *Combray (Illiers)* leading him to write extensively of his experiences there.

Menorah (p.35)

A menorah is a candelabra that holds nine candles, one for each of the eight nights of Hanukkah, and one called the *shammash* to light the other eight. The *shammash* is lit each night, left to burn and replaced nightly with the other candles designated for that night.

Owl as Oboe (p.45)

This poem is "stolen" from Robert Frost's "Dust of Snow." An oboe is used by some orchestras instead of the first violin to sound the tuning "A." because of the stability of its pitch.

Provenance (p.48)

Provenance is documentary evidence for the legitimacy of a work of art. *Grande Jatte* is a painting by George Seurat. He developed a style called pointillism in which small dots of color are arranged in patterns to create an image, like pixels on a screen.

Supervised Injection Sites (p.107)

Apollyon literally means "the Destroyer" in Greek mythology. (Also, Satan. Revelations 9:11). Apollo, among other functions, is the Greek god of healing.

Circumnavigation (p.120)

Francis Chichester was knighted by Queen Elizabeth II for being the first person to sail around the world single-handed on his boat Gypsy Moth IV in 1966-67.

A Perfect Project (p.138)

Eliphaz the Temanite, according to the *Book of Job* in the Hebrew Bible, was the first of three visitors to comfort Job in his sorrows

Without My Cell Phone How Will I Know? (p.152)

"No man ever steps in the same river twice, for it's not the same river and he's not the same man," is an oracular epigram from Heraclitus, the Greek pre-Socratic philosopher, who lived during the Persian empire.

Acknowlegements

Family members, teachers, friends, fellow writers and editors each influenced this collection in ways both large and small. You may not be aware of (and some are no longer here to know) the part you played, but I am. To you each, my gratitude.

Elizabeth Bernstein
Jessica, Chanon, Nicholas, David Bernstein
Barbara Green, Victor H. Bernstein

Arthur Dewing, Alexander Laing, Thomas Vance, Ramon Guthrie, John W. Finch,

Richard Eberhart, T.S.K. Scott-Craig, David Huddle, Gladys LaFlamme Colburn

Randall Weingarten, Mark Schultz, Nancy Nahra, Willard Randall,
Gary Margolis

Rachel Carter, Rachel Fisher, Sofia Silva Wright,
at Onion River Press

Some of the poems published here have appeared in whole or part in poetry journals and other collections including *The Anthology of New England Writers, The Jewish Literary Journal, Dartmouth Literary Magazine, Granite, The Arena*. All copyrights have been reserved by the author.

About the author

Dr. Bernstein's license to practice poetry has run concurrently with his license to practice medicine in Vermont for fifty years. He lives in Jericho with his wife and dogs.

www.ingramcontent.com/pod-product-compliance
Lightning Source LLC
Chambersburg PA
CBHW020251130626
46549CB00005B/2177

SEX

BADDEST SIN OR GOODEST PLEASURE

RON VIESELMEYER

The EC Publishing LLC books may be ordered
through booksellers or by contacting:

EC Publishing LLC
116 South Magnolia Ave.
Suite 3, Unit F
Ocala, FL 34471, USA
Direct Line: +1 (352) 644-6538
Fax: +1 (800) 483-1813
http://www.ecpublishingllc.com/

Ordering Information:
Quantity sales. Special discounts are available on quan-
tity purchases by corporations, associations, and others. For
details, contact the publisher at the address above.

Printed in the United States of America

TABLE OF CONTENTS

DEDICATION

To Kate, my loving wife, who supported me for this past year as I wrestled with ideas in this manuscript. She was my typist and most valuable critic. Most of all, Kate is my partner in life and the inspiration needed to coherently pull my thoughts together to help you the reader better understand the subject matter in this manuscript. She continues in this difficult time through her life-threatening illness to stand with me.

ACKNOWLEDGEMENTS

To my sister Lois and brother-in-law Earl Ambrose for critiquing the original manuscript and giving me valuable input.

To Miranda O'Donnell for page art, and Alissa McKay for typing assistance during final editing.

To Shiree Cosgrove and Cameron Reagon for the book cover design and Del Still for a second opinion regarding content visuals and to Katie Broughton for typing and making corrections to the final submission for publication.

FOREWORD

Dr. Vieselmeyer brings a unique voice in his book. First, he repeatedly reminds us of the tremendous price that is being imposed on Western culture by the trend of decay in sexual mores. The enormity is mind-boggling. Those costs are very real.

Then he ratchets up that point with proof from his counseling experience.

It is one thing to contrast real-life sexual activity of others with the standards set out in Scripture and then project the dire consequences. It is completely another to let those who have chosen or endured alternative standards to engage their own tongues. When they describe the troubles they have experienced, it has particular gravity. Without adopting Biblical standards, his clients prove the troubles associated when people abandon them.

I found it particularly compelling that Ron has counseled those afflicted by their sexual choices or experiences in a practice that has spanned several decades. Changing social mores did not change the need his clients felt for counseling to deal with all those troubles that the Bible proclaims will occur.

Guilt, shame, depression—the list of troubles goes on and on. I hope it will give everyone pause to reconsider the claims and standards set out in the Bible. However, at a minimum, the long list of troubles that Ron's clients recount should move everyone to a point of compassion. We simply cannot turn a blind eye to the damage being imposed by the decay in sexual standards. It is culturally unaffordable both in economic terms and in terms of human tragedy.

Bill Sali
United States Congressman

GOTCHA!

Be honest, why did you decide to scan this book? Why did you take the next step and walk up to the cashier to purchase it? The word SEX got your attention, didn't it? Curiosity caused you to purchase this book.

Instantly upon reading the word SEX on the cover of this book, a broad area of thoughts and emotions surfaced. Visual images and words related to sex strongly affected your whole being, physically, emotionally, socially, spiritually, as well as morally.

What kind of thoughts and feelings you experienced were determined by the kind of sex education, or lack thereof, including actual sexual experiences or exposure from a very early age until the present. Our minds are more vulnerable to pollution in the area of our sexuality than any other area.

Now that I have your attention, stay with me. You are about to obtain information that is extremely relevant for the culture at this time. This is quite possibly one of the most important books you will read on this subject.

SEX—what an incredibly powerful concept! It was perfectly conceived in the mind of the Perfect Designer Creator in eternity past. Perfect is the perfect word to describe God, His character, His person, and His role as Creator. Using the word perfect as it applies to Almighty God is appropriate yet vastly inadequate.

The reason Hollywood and designers of TV commercials sexualize such a high percentage of their programming and advertising is because they know that sex will influence one's thoughts, actions, and emotional responses like no other topic. Unfortunately, too often they push the envelope beyond human decency.

PURPOSE STATEMENT

The purpose for writing on this subject is to show through comparisons there is a better way to experience sexual fulfillment through a healthy marriage. I will be sharing with you how traditional marriage, as designed by the Creator, is superior to the evolutionary theory. Keep in mind that evolution is only a theory with no proof of a workable plan for life (sexuality in particular).

My plan is to develop this subject more fully by showing that due to man's rejection of the Creator, his sexual ideas and practices have failed. In fact, they are destructive to the persons, their marriage, their family, and to society. In contrast, God's plan is wonderfully constructive. While expanding on these thoughts in the ensuing chapters, focus with me on the Creator's principles. When put into practice, they will help you experience a greater measure of fulfillment through marital intimacy. More importantly, I will share with you how you can understand and experience a wonderful, loving intimacy with the Creator Himself.

CHAPTER 1
SEX, A NOVEL IDEA

I started to write this script based on 50+ years of experience as a counselor and a minister, including both formal and informal research. Numerous questions have penetrated my thinking while trying to determine how to tackle this sensitive subject. The most powerful question being asked is, "who designed and created this whole idea of sex and sexuality?" At this point in writing this transcript (although being strongly tempted), I am not going to try to answer this question.

Originally, I had planned to share information about some of my clients regarding their struggles with their sexuality as a result of deviant sexual experiences. Then a novel idea struck me, why not let my clients tell their own stories in their own words. In so doing, the stories are more accurate and powerfully meaningful. Since this is such a sensitive subject and because these people have suffered greatly with anxiety, depression, rejection, anger, guilt, fear, and low self-esteem, I suggested to the writers that they remain anonymous by using fictitious names. A few of those who agreed to write their stories, said they did not care if I used their real name if their testimonies would help someone else who was hurting or was trapped in a sexual addiction. The stories you will read interspersed throughout the book include a variety of sexual issues these clients have been struggling with. Due to the many multifaceted problems, we cannot all relate to every story. However, most of us can relate to several issues.

Over the last 50 years, our culture has embraced and promoted various kinds of deviant sexual activity. The high majority of teenagers and adults in the Western World have had some experience with premarital sex. I think my clients over the years make up a pretty fair sampling of those who have experienced sex outside of marriage. We are no longer bound by puritanical standards.

Perversions are now called "lifestyles" to be celebrated. Whatever we choose to practice, if it feels right, we are told it is right for "me." Psychologists, psychiatrists, and sex therapists have encouraged us to have an open mind and experiment with a variety of sexual experiences and partners both male and female. They say it can be educational, fulfilling, healthy, and has the potential of discovering one's true sexual identity. May I suggest as a counselor, people who involve themselves in these kinds of practices experience physical, emotional, social, mental, and spiritual problems. The deterioration of morality is happening with such rapidity as never before seen or experienced in the history of the world. Some of the news items and stories in this book have taken place during the writing of this manuscript. As previously stated, those of liberal philosophy and evolutionary theory call this an exciting, progressive development on the stage of history.

Yet God who created the universe, the earth, and all of its inhabitants, especially man whom He made to rule over His creation said, "It was good." God is broken-hearted because man has rejected Him, exchanged good for evil, and is destroying God's beautiful plan of intimate relationships with our fellowman and consequently God Himself. We are told that emotionally and mentally these experiences are healthy and freeing. A large segment of society has bought into this liberal philosophy as being acceptable and normal when one is ready. When is one ready? They say when it feels right, it is OK to have sex. Ready is a relative theory. My question is, "Why do those who practice this kind of behavior suffer with guilt?" In addition, it must be understood that guilt is the number one cause of depression. Young women and teenage girls who are sexually active will more openly exhibit anxiety and depression than men and teenage boys.

Females share their thoughts and feelings with friends and/or family members. Change in attitude and behavior should cause concern to those who are close to the teenage girl. Frequently, they will demonstrate bizarre behaviors such as cutting themselves and/or eating disorders.

Usually their self-esteem goes down while they are sexually active. Often they turn to alcohol and/or non-prescribed drugs hoping that it will minimize their emotional pain. However, it only brings temporary relief followed by despair which results in self-destructive behaviors, such as suicidal thoughts and too often manifesting itself in suicide attempts. Often a girl's confidence and self-image are bolstered by a handsome young man who makes her feel important, while his real intent is selfishly to engage her in sexual intimacy. Often the same young man destroys her self-worth when he gets her pregnant or ignores her in favor of the next cute girl who comes along.

It has often been stated, "It ain't fair that boys always get away with it." This has been called the double standard. In the past, there has been a lot of truth to this theory. However, with the feminist movement of the last 40 years or so, women and teenage girls have asserted themselves, often taking the initiative in sexual relationships.

Recently I read a bumper sticker that said, "Feminism is the radical idea that women are human." Unfortunately, throughout history too many men have treated women inhumanely. In some countries, the demeaning treatment of women is a cultural practice. Sometimes misapplied religion plays a role in the dominant control men have over women. Regrettably, with the aggressive behavior related to the feminist movement many young women have played a role in lowering their own self-esteem.

Now, let me share from a male and a counselor's perspective my insight regarding men and teenage boys' experiences resulting from the double standard. Men are mostly to blame for their own self-destructive behavior. Just as men through rejection cause women's self-esteem to go down, women also through rejection play a role in the lowering of a man's self-esteem.

Men who take advantage of women and girls sexually also suffer from insecurity, anger, anxiety, guilt, and depression. I mentioned earlier that women are more likely to share with someone what is going on in their lives emotionally than men are. Boys from a very early age are taught to hold their feelings in. It usually starts when the little boy is approximately two years of age. The little guy falls down and skins his knee. He starts to cry (I think we would all agree this is normal behavior). Someone (usually the father, older brother, or another male, occasionally the mother) says, "Don't cry, you are a big boy." What happens if a little girl skins her knee? Mom kisses it and makes it better. What happens the next time the little boy gets hurt? He goes to Mom, Dad, or whoever is available, shows them his owie and while fighting back tears says, "It hurts, but I didn't crrrrry. I'm a big boy." Boys from an early age learn they are supposed to be macho. They are supposed to pull themselves together and act as if it doesn't hurt. Boys being boys often get into fights. They hurt each other, but they won't tell how bad it hurts. They just try to inflict more pain on the other one.

When I was younger, I played some contact sports. There were times I got hurt, but I didn't let anyone know how much it hurt, especially the opposing team. Both of my sons were football players. They were banged up pretty good from time to time. I will never forget the time we traveled 3000 miles to watch a game when our oldest son was playing for WestPoint the Armed Forces Military Academy. The day before the game, he injured his wrist in a scrimmage. He didn't tell his coach or us how badly he was injured. He wanted us to see him play. After the game, he admitted he had played with a lot of pain. Kate, my wife, his mother who is a nurse, determined he should have it x-rayed. We found out he had played with a broken wrist. Being an athletic family, we have attended numerous sporting events. It is obvious that girls' behavior when they are injured is different from boys. While boys hold their feelings in, girls verbally express their feelings. I share these illustrations to show you that boys and girls deal with pain differently, including emotional pain.

In most cases, when a teenage boyfriend-girlfriend relationship breaks up there is considerable hurt. Girls usually cry and tell their friends. Boys generally hold it all in. If they cry, they do it when they are alone. The same is true with husband and wife when a marriage breaks up. If the couple decides to seek help, more than 8 times out of 10 the wife is the one who calls the counselor. The macho husband says we don't need a counselor, we can handle it on our own. Both psychologists and medical doctors tell us that if we bottle up our emotions it affects our physical well-being. While men deal differently with conflict, they do no escape the consequences of their behavior. Both males and females struggle with suicidal thoughts and attempts due to depression caused by guilt. However, men are more likely to succeed in taking their lives. There has been considerable discussion coupled with research trying to determine why women live approximately six years longer than men do. I have my own theory.

I believe men in the Western culture die earlier because they have learned from an early age to bury their feelings, especially guilt feelings. Many psychologists and numerous counselors have told their clients who are dealing with guilt to just forgive themselves. Unfortunately, it does not work. The only way we can experience forgiveness is by asking the Creator (who made the rules) and the persons' we have hurt by our sinful, self-defeating behavior for forgiveness.

CHAPTER 2

FREE SEX

America has been labeled "The Land of the Free" (The culture of the free society). Back in the 60's and 70's, Berkeley, San Francisco, and Woodstock became the forerunners of the era of adulterated relativism. Liberal philosophers promoted freethinking, including the use of mind-altering drugs, and free sex. Absolute moral truths were mocked, ridiculed, and disregarded. Like a bunch of lemmings, college aged students who were desperately seeking answers for life fell in lock step behind the liberal professors and their do-your-own-thing philosophy.

In the Old Testament, at a time in history when man turned his back on God, we read every man did that which right in his own eyes. Often referred to as *unrestricted freedom*. Reality is we lose our freedom when we ignore God and do it our way.

The secular evolutionists, anti-God people are working overtime doing everything in their power to take God out of the equation. Without God, there are no convictions or moral rules to follow. In the 70's when free sex was having an impact on every aspect of society, I was writing an essay on the subject of the Homosexual Matrix. As part of my research I wanted to know what role religion played, if any, in slowing the inroads of sexual activity outside of marriage. I discovered there was very little difference between the religious and the non-religious. I interviewed the pastor of a large, conservative church. He told me they were desperate for answers. He said they had six ministers on staff. During the prior year, they had performed numerous wedding ceremonies, and every couple had been sexually active before the wedding. They all wanted a church wedding or at least a member of the clergy to perform the ceremony.

I asked him WHY? He said, "Because they wanted God's blessing on their marriage." He said that most of those for whom they had performed the ceremony returned for counseling during the first year of marriage. What they didn't seem to understand is that God's blessing is the result of obeying God's rules, in this situation, obedience in the matter of sexuality. Webster defines blessing as "a statement of divine favor." God will not bestow His favor on those who disregard and refuse to obey His laws, His commandments, and His principles.

I was involved in campus ministry on major universities and college campuses across the U.S. and Canada. Periodically when talking about sin there would be a heckler in the audience who tried to make a mockery of sin. At that point, I often asked the students in the audience to define sin. Most of the time in their responses, they said it had something to do with sex, sometimes referring to Adam and Eve being naked and eating an apple. Recently I attended a conference on "The Steeling of the Mind". Later while working on this manuscript, I began thinking about how one's mind can so easily be skewed in regards to sex. Frankly, I do not know of any other aspect of a person's life where the mind is more easily polluted than in the area of a person's sexuality.

Sexual sins are the most potent and persistent sins of the mind. Proverbs 23:7 says, *"As a man thinketh in his heart, so is he."* Prior to the free sex generation, reference to sex in the media was almost non-existent. Now there is hardly ever a late night show where there isn't reference made to or jokes made about sex. Sex on the sitcoms has become the dominant norm. Abnormal sex has become the brunt of jokes and mockery of that which God intended to be beautiful, enjoyable, and wonderfully fulfilling. Much of society has embraced the idea that the words traditional, normal, and natural no longer have the same meaning. Traditional norms are no longer applicable when it comes to sex related issues.

Since I will be referring from time to time to these words and a few other words that people do not want to hear such as abnormal, unnatural, deviant, and perverted when it comes to their own personal sexual expression, I feel it necessary to define some of these words according to Webster:

Deviant: Departing from the norm; a person who departs markedly from the accepted norm.

Pervert: To lead astray morally; to turn away from the right course; to turn to an improper use; a person who practices a sexual perversion; debase.

Perverted: An unnatural or abnormal nature; turn from what is considered right or true.

Vile: Wretchedly bad; highly offensive; unpleasant; objectionable; morally debased; despicable.

I cannot emphasize enough that free sex is NOT FREE. In fact, it is the opposite of freedom. Bondage is the consequence of sex outside of God's plan. Sexual freedom does not mean doing whatever you please with any willing partner. **Sexual freedom results from using sex within the bonds of marriage the way God intended.** Take a moment to pause, and really contemplate that last sentence.

My daughter shared with me her experience in presenting her proposal for her dissertation to a group of nine Ph.D.s. This brought back memories of 39 years ago when I submitted my proposal. The title of my dissertation proposal was 'Mass Hysteria-The Lemming Syndrome'. The council did not look at my topic favorably. One councilor in particular did not look at my subject matter as being relevant. He suggested I research and write on the subject of 'Substance Abuse in the Work Place'. While he did not insist that I write on his suggested topic, he made me feel guilty for not wanting to take his advice. Eventually, I reluctantly took his advice to keep him happy and hopefully upon completion he would approve the finished product.

Over the years, periodically I would think about my desire to write on 'Mass Hysteria' when circumstances arose that made me realize how applicable and relevant my original subject of choice was. The Lemming Syndrome shows us how easily large masses of people follow leaders who lead them down the path of destruction. Just in my lifetime, I can think of a number of philosophies and misguided religious leaders who have played major roles in the downfall and destruction of cultures and countries.

The following is a short list: Fascism, Marxism, Communism, Socialism, and now Progressivism. The following are a few of the leaders: Stalin, Hitler, Mussolini, Khrushchev plus numerous dictators around the world.

You asked what does the 'Lemming Syndrome' have to do with the subject of this book, and in particular this chapter? Again, in my lifetime perverted sexual immorality has come out from behind closed doors. The media, educational institutions, governments, and even some religious leaders and institutions have gone public in support of sexual immorality. Millions of people, just like lemmings, have hurriedly fallen in line and are practicing same sex marriages. Millions more who are not actually practicing homosexuality embrace and support those who do.

And yes, this behavior is rapidly destroying our culture.

Each generation since liberal philosophers, professors, theologians, politicians, attorneys, and judges have continued to push the envelope a little bit further to the left. Progressives continue to move to the left in their experimenting with and practicing sexual immorality.

Alan Keyes said, "We must restore the moral basis of our own self-control and our own self-respect. Without it, we will surrender all of our liberties. Society has the right to hold people responsible for their moral behavior."

The *Bible* also clearly warns us to guard against the sin of sexual immorality, and protect ourselves from the consequence of sin by being obedient, self-controlled, and choosing to preserve God's beautiful plan for our lives. God's Word is very clear.

"For this is the will of God, ...that you abstain from sexual immorality." 1 Thessalonians 4:3

"The body is not meant for sexual immorality, but for the Lord." 1 Corinthians 6:13

"Let us walk properly as in the daytime, not in orgies and drunkenness, not in sexual immorality and sensuality, ...but put on the Lord Jesus Christ, and make no provision for the flesh, to gratify its desires." Romans 13: 13-14

CHAPTER 3

IRRESPONSIBLE SEX

The promoters of the sexual revolution are playing a leading role in the reshaping of our culture. In certain parts of the country, especially areas where young people are underemployed, they are trying to find acceptance and an identity. Due to much idleness, they are finding a measure of acceptance in sexual activity. All too often, the young girls get pregnant. The young father who has never learned responsibility disappears. The young girl then finds her identity in being a mother, she has not been taught skills in motherhood, and she is still living at home. Her mother takes on most of the responsibility in raising the baby. A high percentage of the time these young mothers do not marry. Often they repeat the scenario by getting pregnant again, and more often than not, by a different father. In some areas, single parenthood is as high as 72 percent and the custodial parent is usually the mother. These babies grow up in a dysfunctional family, but this is all they know. Dysfunction seems normal to them. When the babies become teenagers, they live what they were modeled, and follow in the footsteps of their mothers.

These young mothers learn quickly from their mothers and the Department of Health and Welfare that they will be taken care of financially. They receive welfare checks, housing allowance, free medical, food stamps, and free breakfast and lunches through the school system. The drain on the economy, (costs to the taxpayer) is astronomical. We make it too easy to obtain welfare support. Some of my welfare clients refer to their welfare checks as paychecks. There should be more emphasis put on educating both young males and females, through the schools, churches, and other community programs. They need to learn self-discipline and responsibility, especially when it comes to sexual behavior. There should also be consequences for irresponsible behavior. Consequences can be a valuable means to learning responsibility.

While valuable lessons are learned from experience, some experiences such as the passing around of sexually transmitted diseases are destructive and can be life-altering to individuals. Not only do high school and college students get involved mutually in sexual practices while dating, sometimes sexual activity results in rape, the unwanted violation of one's body and psyche. Last night the subject on 48 Hours was about students being molested by teachers, both male and female. The interviewer said this problem is of epidemic proportions. It is estimated that 7% of students have been molested by a teacher.

The following statistics were published in the July 18, 2014 issue of the Idaho Statesman. In epidemic numbers, gonorrhea cases grew by 50 percent in three months. In the five Northern Idaho counties, the area where I live, cases jumped by 300 percent in 2013. According to the State Health Department records, Chlamydia is also increasing rapidly. According to the U.S. Center for Disease Control and Prevention, almost half of all American high school students admit to having had sexual intercourse. CDC reports that one in four U.S. teen girls has contracted at least one sexually transmitted disease, and every day in America, approximately 10,000 teenagers contract a sexually transmitted disease. History has shown us that a sexually immoral permissive society is a major cause for the decline of the culture.

A national obsession with sex is leading to a moral decline of society. Richard D. Land served for 25 years as president of the Ethics and Religious Liberty Commission of the Southern Baptist Convention. He said, "Frankly, the sexual revolution has done more damage to this country than anything else ever has." Sexual moral decline has become an ignored, deadly pandemic afflicting society. It is highly infectious; it is highly infectious, and spreading rapidly with each passing year.

While growing up, my siblings and I were taught that we were to treat the office of President with respect. However, in the last few years the men and women hold high offices have chosen to disrespect and denigrate the office of President.

Regarding the subject matter of this book, Presidents Clinton, Obama, and Biden have shown a complete lack of respect for the American citizens. In his responsibility as Commander in Chief of the United States Armed Forces. He by his actions has made it clear that his first priority was to embrace and support homosexuals. He signed an executive order that encourages homosexuals to come out of the closet (go public) with their deviant lifestyle. Recently, the President made personal calls to athletes who have come out of the closet, congratulating them for their courage. In addition, recently he made the statement that evil can be eradicated, but it would happen slowly over a period of time. My question is how can you promote immorality (evil) and eradicate evil at the same time?

The Obama administration granted an array of new benefits to same sex couples, including those who live in states where homosexual marriage is against the law.

Overriding the states and the will of the people is a slap in the face to the majority of Americans, especially the military personnel who have sacrificed so much to protect and preserve our freedom. They are not even allowed to voice their honest opinions about homosexuality. If they do, they may have to answer to the powers that be for speaking the truth. Not only is our President promoting evil behavior, his actions in promoting his agenda are dictatorial at its best.

Recent news is that the Social Security Administration will start processing some survivor death benefits for those in same sex relationships who live in states that don't recognize homosexual marriage, even though court challenges to gay marriage bans are still pending in several states.

Recently, a Malaysian Airplane was shot down by a Russian missile killing all 298 people aboard. On July 18, 2014, President Obama spoke to the American people and the world offering words of concern, sympathy, and support, especially to those who lost loved ones. The problems in the Ukraine and the Middle East are extremely serious issues. However, toward the end of his speech he again offered his support for same sex unions and asked us, the American people, to join him by supporting people who are sexually different. Regardless of our beliefs about sexual deviancy, this was an inappropriate time to promote his agenda of support for this issue.

January 12th, 2016 President Obama gave his final State of the Union address in his speech, twice he boastfully touted his accomplishment of same-sex marriage. He said, "Americans can now marry whomever they love."

There was no mention of same-sex marriage by any of the previous Presidents. President Obama seems to find a way to take advantage of every opportunity to force his immoral agenda on the American people.

Abraham Lincoln while calling for a national day of prayer and fasting during the American Civil War said, "We have been the recipients of the choicest bounties of Heaven; we have been preserved these many years in peace and prosperity; we have grown in numbers, wealth, and power as no other nation has ever grown. But we have forgotten God …And we have vainly imagined, in the deceitfulness of our hearts, that all these blessings were produced by some superior wisdom and virtue of our own…It behooves us, then, to humble ourselves before the offended Power, to confess our national sins and to pray for clemency and forgiveness." Quoted by William Federer, America's God and Country Encyclopedia of Quotations, 1996, pp. 383-384.

CHAPTER 4
BRAINWASHED

During the last 40 years, society has brainwashed us with all kinds of propaganda via the media and liberal educators. They argue that a loving God would not expect us to have to wait until we are married to enjoy sexual intimacy. I had a 40-year-old single mom tell me that having to wait until you are married to have sex is discrimination against single people, especially against those who choose not to marry.

People with this philosophy choose to reject God's plan. In so doing, they have no absolute standard to guide and protect them from the numerous consequences of irresponsible behavior. Do they really think that they can improve on God's plan and avoid the consequences? They say they are acting responsibly by protecting themselves from sexually transmitted diseases and unwanted pregnancies by using condoms, or other methods of protection and birth control.

Colleges and numerous public schools encourage sexual activity by providing free condoms. Too often men, women, and teenage girls and boys are willing to take a chance with no protection, or at the very least minimal precautions for the sake of instant gratification. Because of the trust people place in condoms, there are numerous variations of sexual cohabitating relationships. Often these relationships lead to confusing ever-changing situations for children.

The safety of women and children depend upon marital stability. Cohabitating, unmarried women are more likely than married women to suffer physical and sexual abuse. The consequences of cohabitation are even more serious for the children. The most unsafe of all family environments is that in which the mother is living with someone other than the child's biological father. Stable marital unions promote the health, safety, and social progress of women, men, and children due to the power of family values and support. Without it, many say after it is too late, "If only, I wish I had, or I should have." Broken lives are the result of, "Why should I wait, or I can't wait."

The percentage of dating couples who are having sex before marriage is extremely high. Our culture from parents, sex education in the public schools, information through the media, etc., has communicated to us that when two people are ready, sexual intimacy is normal. My question is, when is one ready? My experience and knowledge tell me most boys are ready by twelve years of age. Most girls are ready when peer pressure by boyfriends and sexually active girlfriends send a message that it is better to have sex with your boyfriend than to lose him or be made fun of by her peers for wanting to cherish her virginity.

To make the teenagers feel more comfortable about their decision to become sexually active, sex education teachers tell them it is normal and healthy to experiment. To help them feel safer, their teachers tell them where they can obtain condoms. Some of these teachers have lobbied the school board to make condoms available through the schools. Some even want to make the morning after pill available.

If being ready is the determining factor as to when to choose to become sexually active, then why is it statutory rape for an 18-year-old to have sex with a consenting 16-year-old? I guess maturity has some merit. However, sometimes the 16-year-old is more mature than the 18-year-old. This may sound a bit sarcastic! However, if consent is a determining factor, perhaps if one wants to have sex outside of marriage the consent should come from one's spouse, children, parents, brothers, sisters, friends and neighbors. There would be considerably fewer fornicators, adulterers, broken marriages, destroyed families, and single parents. Also there would be less poverty.

The supporters of free sex try to convince us that along with mutual consent it is OK to be sexually active as long as we are not hurting other people. The problem with this theory is it is impossible to commit sexual sin without it affecting one or more other people. All sexual sin is against God and humanity. Modern day society is a direct result of sin having entered the world thousands of years ago, and generations have just fanned the flame.

This article by the Associated Press appeared in our local newspaper recently.

Experts Offer New Sex Ed Guidelines
Minimum standards presented:

Young elementary school students should use the proper names for body parts, and by the end of the 5th grade know that sexual orientation is "the romantic attraction of an individual to someone of the same gender or a different gender," according to new sexual education guidelines released by a coalition of health and education groups.

It is interesting how they put the emphasis on deviant sexual behavior first, but avoid calling it deviant. Regardless of how much we downplay sexual immorality, our consciences will not allow us to escape the consequences of our behavior. Perhaps it would be better to try the Creator's ideal instead.

CHAPTER 5
PREGNANCY OUTSIDE OF MARRIAGE

I hope that the following story will help answer some of your questions about the consequences of pregnancy outside of marriage that culminates in abortion.

Ross and Teri's Story

Ross and I decided we wanted to have children. After a year of testing the doctor discovered I had polyps that needed to be removed. My doctor said there should be absolutely no reason for us not to get pregnant. Our quest to have children began anew, with fresh hope. Every month would bring emotional pain when my cycle would start. WHY? Why were we not getting pregnant? My doctor had no answers for us – his next suggestion was that I be placed on fertility drugs.

We had become so discouraged and emotionally drained. The thought of going through the process was overwhelming. After discussions with a doctor who specializes in fertility issues, we went ahead with fertility medication. The emotional devastation of a want-to-be Dad and Mom at the end of the allowable limit of fertility medication, with no positive pregnancy, was heart wrenching.

The only thing left is to recommend in-vitro fertilization. We decided the longing in our hearts for children could endure "one more thing." We went to Lake City to meet with the specialist.

She said that in-vitro fertilization was not only costly, but could be emotionally draining. She did not want to take any chances. Ross and I could see her reasoning. However, with renewed hope, I yielded to taking the tests.

During the preliminary testing, she discovered why I could not get pregnant. I was born with a deformity. Everything in me said, "I can't take it anymore." Yet with resignation, I submitted to surgery to correct the problem. The surgery was a success and my doctor was ecstatic.

When it was time to go for my two-month follow-up, I was having some discomfort. I thought something must be wrong with the healing. They did a pregnancy test at the doctor's office. We discovered I was pregnant. Unbelievable – Hallelujah!

Fast forward – it was the final week. Everything was looking great. The culmination of the last 7 years was about to be birthed into our lives. My parents came. They wanted to participate in the celebration of their only daughter's baby coming into the world after having been through so much. That evening we were going to bed and I notice that the baby had been quiet for some time. We decided to go to the hospital. We were entirely silent during the trip. We went to the Labor and Delivery area. A technician hooked me to the monitor. We knew from the look on his face – he didn't even have to say it – but he did. "I cannot find a heartbeat." As Ross and I lay there and heard the words, the only life thread we had was ripped from our very souls. It was at this opportune moment that the accuser came to visit me.

His words were quite simple, but very effective. "You know you deserve this. You know that your God is punishing you." For you see, we had made the decision to have an abortion earlier in our courtship. Prior to our getting married, we had done what I knew to be the consummate sin. We had made the horrifying choice of death for our child. It was not easily made. Ross had decided to move back to his home to try to forget about me. There were times when I would call him and tell him not to call me, to forget me, and I would not contact him anymore.

I went to the abortion clinic, I remember quite clearly the nurse physically pushing me down, and turning the monitor away from me as I had raised up to see what she was seeing on the screen. She assured me that it was all right. I would have no problem having children again. This was an OK, easy thing to do. If it is so easy, why did I feel so horrible? Why was I crying all the time? Why was I an emotional wreck??

And so the enemy had me. It was with glee that he watched us writhe in pain and agony in that hospital that night. Oh how right he was, we were in fact being punished for our horrible act. We would die and never have the hope of seeing our daughter laugh and cry and live. We would never have the hope of one day being united with her because of what we had done. I asked numerous questions of a caring friend. How do I get right with God? How can I possibly be forgiven? Our poor friend finally said I don't have the answer to your questions but I know someone who does, would you mind if I gave him your number. Absolutely not, we said. After all, we were desperate to see our daughter. God had reached down through this friend and gave us hope.

It was through this faithful, willing servant that God came to visit us in our home. That faithful, willing servant was a pastor. There we were lying on our bed; I was recovering from a C-section and my husband had just had back surgery. We were grief stricken and desperate. Pastor Todd tenderly answered all our questions, and even though we did not share with him our abortion past, God knew. Pastor Todd would listen to our questions and say, I know why you asked that question, and then he would share from his heart. What really spoke to us that day was the truth of God and His Son Jesus Christ. Every time Pastor Todd shared from his heart, he would open his Bible and share the heart of God through Scripture.

It was three weeks after the death of our daughter that I heard the sweet truth from God. That I not only could be forgiven, but that I could indeed be united with our daughter in Heaven. Jesus Christ who shed His blood on Calvary was our passport out of hell, not only the eternal hell but also the hell we experience here on earth. I received Jesus Christ as my Savior that day, also my husband surrendered to Christ.

God has done amazing things in our lives. God has blest me with the opportunity to exchange the mantle of death I carried to the mantle of Life. I now have the privilege of being a volunteer at Life Line Crisis Pregnancy Center. God has allowed my life's story to impact others for you see it really isn't a story about my life it is about His Life, about His forgiveness, His redemption, about His loving kindness, it's about His Grace, about His mercy, and it is about His divine healing.

Ross and Teri

CHAPTER 6

ABORTION

The previous story is further evidence that there are consequences to our actions. When women or teenage girls get pregnant at a time when a baby is not wanted, they lose the joy of expectancy and excitement. They also lose the freedom of a clear conscience. They are not free to govern their own lives. The pregnancy and eventual birth of a baby controls their time, their finances, their planning for the future, and even their thought life. When the baby is not wanted, it becomes a burden. Anger is a huge problem because often the father disappears from the scene. If he doesn't disappear, he refuses to accept responsibility. The mother feels so alone.

Planned Parenthood, the father, other members of the family, the doctor, and friends often try to convince the mother that there is a simple quick fix; remove the unwanted baby by way of an abortion. They are told that once the child has been removed, they can get on with their lives. That is a lie. Ask any woman who has had an abortion. The memory of that child and that decision <u>never go away</u>.

Having an abortion also has an impact emotionally and spiritually on the lives of those who perform abortions or assist in performing abortions. I have counseled with two nurses who assisted in performing abortions. Their stories along with testimonies of a few others, who used to be involved in the abortion industry, opened my eyes to the gruesomeness of forcefully terminating pregnancies. It is time for society to get honest about abortion and start labeling it for what it is; MURDER!

We have spent a considerable amount of time discussing the pros and cons of abortion and the impact it has on society. We talked about the effects abortion has on the mothers physically, psychologically, and spiritually. However, we do not say enough about the horrendous experiences the babies go through in the process of being murdered. I suggest you read Monica Miller's book "Abandoned." The mothers should be knowledgeable of the various gruesome procedures used in aborting their babies. All mothers contemplating having an abortion should be required to view a video of the barbaric procedures used to abort babies prior to their final decision. The mothers should be knowledgeable of how the baby is dismembered as its body parts are sucked out of the womb with a vacuum. They should be required to see how the abortionist forces scissors into the back of the baby's skull and how the bodies of innocent babies are burned inside and out when chemicals are used to abort the baby.

Spokane hosts the annual Bloomsday Race. Approximately 50,000 participants compete in this event annually. For the past two years, a group of Pro-life supporters placed a few pictures of aborted babies along the race route. During the evening news, a few people complained about the pictures. In verbalizing their complaints, they used words such as offensive, reprehensible, gruesome, and repugnant. Those who described the pictures asked that something be done to have them removed. They also used disparaging comments when speaking about the Pro-life supporters. It must be understood that there would be no pictures if it weren't for the deplorable, gruesome murders of innocent babies.

I was invited on two occasions to speak at the Annual Northwest Birthright Convention. The topic given to me was "The Psychological Effect of An Abortion." My research substantiated that 100% of women who have had an abortion experience depression. In addition, the evidence supports my personal and informal research as a counselor. A substantial percentage of the women who have had an abortion have suicidal thoughts and some of them attempt suicide. The following are a few thoughts I shared at the convention.

There are four major causes of depression: Chemical depression is the result of the body's chemistry being thrown out of balance by the procedure and/or the use of non-prescribed drugs. A second cause of depression is a loss in a person's life. It could be the death of someone very close to us. Separations in relationships, divorce, etc., can cause depression. Other losses such as the loss of a job, financial security, loss of body functions (sight, hearing, loss of limbs, etc.) can also cause depression.

A third cause is repressed anger. Often the mother feels anger toward the father of the baby. She feels angry toward the doctor who performed the abortion and other people who encouraged her to have the abortion. Usually the mother feels some anger toward herself for getting pregnant and/or allowing the abortion.

The number one cause of depression is guilt. I have yet to counsel with a woman who has had an abortion who didn't experience guilt. All women who have had an abortion experience some depression from all four of the major causes of depression. Women who have had an abortion experience down days on anniversary dates such as the date the baby was aborted, the date the baby would have been born if carried to term, other memory dates such as birthdays of other children she gave life to.

As you can see, the progression of behavior and circumstances lead to a series of consequences often starting with sex outside of God's plan. After speaking at each conference, I made myself available for questions and further personal discussion. Each time there were approximately a dozen women lined up to speak with me. Every one of them had had two or more abortions. One woman had eight abortions, and another woman had six. Most of the women had two to four abortions. All of them said if they had known that having the abortion was the main cause of their depression, they would not have terminated the pregnancy. Some of them said members of the medical profession, Planned Parenthood, or a counselor said carrying an unplanned baby was the cause of their depression. A few of them said they were told it was guilt placed on them by their family or friends. In one case, the gal said society as a whole caused her depression.

Planned Parenthood has set itself up as a caring organization that has women's best interests at heart regarding health issues. Yet in America 1 out of 4 pregnancies end in abortion. According to U.S. News and

World Report, 92 percent of all women who use Planned Parenthood Services get an abortion. For every 145 abortions they perform, Planned Parenthood makes only one adoption referral. In order for this so-called caring organization to carry out women's health services, they receive 540 million dollars a year from us, the taxpayers. In other words, we are paying Planned Parenthood to kill babies,

In addition, Planned Parenthood uses our money to attack Hobby Lobby for the stand they have taken in favor of morality and against abortion. Along with the murdering of babies, all aspects of abortion place a tremendous burden on the economy.

Recently Planned Parenthood was caught selling aborted baby body parts.

CHAPTER 7

PORNOGRAPHY-DANGEROUS BEHAVIOR

The secular liberal proponents and users of pornography have tried to make us believe that pornography is innocent entertainment. They are WRONG! This has been evident in the lives of hundreds of my clients over the years as well as in my personal experience. I had a personal experience that of which I am ashamed. Having grown up on a dairy farm in Southern Idaho, I never enjoyed living in a big city. We were living in Toronto, Ontario, Canada due to the ministry I was involved in. My sons were four and six years of age. I always wanted them to experience farm life. An opportunity arose where I could rent an old farmhouse in a beautiful location. Maple trees lined both sides of the long driveway. Near the house was a beautiful pond surrounded by weeping willow trees. The house had been vacant for several months.

It had not been cleaned since the last tenant moved out. There were large piles of garbage in the kitchen, dining, and living rooms. There were lots of beer cans and liquor bottles. Mixed in with the garbage was a significant amount of pornographic materials. I borrowed a wheelbarrow and a shovel and started hauling the garbage out to the garbage pit and burn barrel. Upon seeing the pornography, out of curiosity, I looked at a few pictures and read a few portions before burning the pornographic magazines and books.

Pornography had never been a part of my life. However, for the next four or five months, I was haunted with perverted memories. I struggled to get the images of graphic pictures and words out of my mind. I suffered with a lot of guilt and shame. I prayed and prayed, asking God to forgive me and to remove those perverted images and thoughts from my mind. After a period of approximately five months, I experienced God's forgiveness. It was like being set free and having a tremendous weight lifted from my shoulders. Part of the process of freeing my mind from these evil thoughts was to listen to wholesome music and read good pure literature. I guess the only good that has come out of my experience is that I can relate to my clients who struggle with an addiction to pornography. In so doing, I am able to offer them hope and help them find deliverance.

Internet pornography coupled with cybersex is the number one addiction in the Western culture. Pornography is a multi-billion-dollar industry. Due to false interpretation of the U.S. Constitution pertaining to freedom of speech, we have not been able to shut down the industry. It is time the producers, the consumers, Congress, and the courts accept responsibility, do what is right, and shut down the supply of addict's so-called entertainment.

While child pornography is illegal, people with perverted minds continue to traffic in and purchase millions of dollars of heinous child pornography exploiting innocent children. The following is an article printed in the Coeur d'Alene Press. The headline reads:

Seventy-one People Charged with Child Porno

Seemingly, respectable members of the mainstream—police officer, a paramedic, a rabbi, an airline pilot, an architect, a Boy Scout leader— were caught using the internet to collect and trade child pornography, federal officials said.

The six were among 70 New York City—area men and one woman charged as a result of a five-week investigation by the Homeland Security Investigation Arm of U.S. Immigration and Customs Enforcement. Some of the defendants, using such terms like "real child rape" and "family sex" had downloaded thousands of disturbing images in their computers. The lone woman was accused of allowing another suspect to videotape her son.

Federal and State officials who announced the arrests called it one of the largest roundups ever of people who seek to anonymously share the porn online—a stark reminder that they come from all walks of life.

Thirty-nine years ago, I had another personal experience. I was working with Open Air Campaigners doing street evangelism in Los Angeles and Hollywood. We used mobile units equipped with platforms, sound systems, and portable sketch boards with lighting. There were only certain locations we were allowed to park these specially equipped vans. One Friday evening we were parked in downtown L.A. I was on the platform sharing the Gospel with an audience of approximately 60 people. There was a man standing directly in front of me listening intently. When I finished speaking, he stepped forward and said he wanted to talk with me. He told me his life was in shambles and he needed answers. He was depressed and suicidal.

He kept looking back toward the building that was on the opposite side of the sidewalk. All of a sudden he said, "I've got to go, a customer just entered my store. Why don't you come in? I want to continue this conversation." I started to follow him. I didn't know until then that his place of business was An Adult Only Store. I felt very awkward wondering what I should do. Before I had a chance to process my dilemma, I found myself following him into the store. Just as I walked through the door, a squeamish, dirty feeling came over me. There were full colored nude pictures of people in provocative sexual poses. Back to our discussion, he told me he hated what he was doing, and he hated himself for assisting people in their perverted addictions. After his customer left, we went outside.

Later in our conversation, I said to him, "I have been here for over two hours and you have had only one customer. How do you make a living doing this?" He told me that most of his business was mail order. Most of his male walk-in customers came in after 1 a.m. and most of his female customers come in midday during the week. I was always under the opinion that pornography and deviant sex practices were committed mostly by men. He told me that the percentage of women who have sex addictions is almost as high as with men. He said women are just better at hiding their sex addictions, just as they are better at concealing alcohol and drug addictions.

A modern day type of pornography is sexting. This kind of behavior in many ways is considerably more dangerous because younger and younger children and teenagers practice it. It is just as damaging to the psyche as so-called mature adult pornography. The subjects of adult pornography are anonymous. The subjects of sexting are usually friends or other people that are known by the one who is doing the sexting.

When the images are of people that you know it is almost impossible to forget what one has seen. The younger one is when he or she gets involved in various kinds of pornography, the more likely they are to become addicted. Snuff movies and hard-core pornography play into the hands of organized crime.

While speaking with one man who was addicted to hard-core pornography he referred to his life as pure hell. If this is a problem in your life, you must do everything possible to break the addiction and memories and invite the support of family and friends. As with alcohol and substance abuse there is a monetary cost to society resulting from days off work, sick leave, and higher insurance premiums. Progressives support more benefits for people with immorality addictions. Pornography corrupts minds, destroys marriages and families. Sexually oriented businesses play on peoples' vulnerabilities and corrupt neighborhoods via video and convenience stores.

CHAPTER 8
PEDOPHILIA

Pedophiles are experts at enticing children to get into their automobile or come into their home. They make promises to children to break down their resistance before molesting them. This is followed by more promises and threats if they tell somebody. Often they threaten to harm the child's parents if the child reports the pedophile. Consequences to having been sexually abused as a child are the inability to trust. Their inability to trust can last a lifetime. Also, a very high percentage of women and some men find it hard to properly respond sexually later on in marriage.

The following is a story of an abused young boy:

Corey's Story

My abuse took place when I was nine years old. We had moved to a small town just west of Raton. Behind our house was a little farm with horses. Behind the house was an old barn with a hayloft. I don't remember how I meet Stan, but he was a cool guy. He was in high school and he loved to play with me. Any high school guy who would spend time with a little guy, like me, was the coolest in the world.

I saw Stan almost every day after school. We would play outside and in the hayloft. We would play board games, like Monopoly. I came to trust Stan very quickly and he knew it. It wasn't long before our play time evolved into something dark – sinister. Stan told me he wanted to start treating me like a high school guy and that he wanted to show me what high school kids did. He would ask me, "You want to be cool, don't you?" What all Stan asked me to do in order to be "cool" is not necessary to put in this story. Just know this, for six months I was sexually abused by a young man that lured me into his lair and took advantage of a little, nine-year old boy.

Growing up was difficult for me, especially growing up in church. I never felt particularly good about myself, but I never connected it to the abuse. Although I would not have called it "gay" – that word meant "happy" when I was a child – I was confused about sexuality. No one ever talked to me about sex – not my parents, teachers, the pastor – no one. Pornography was a huge part of my abuse, so I knew what a woman looked like. And I knew about the act of sex or intercourse. I even was very familiar with "self-fulfillment." I had a difficult time with understanding intimacy, love, and relationships.

In my experience, sex was with a magazine and was all about me; it made me feel good and awful – mostly awful and confused. Later in my life, I discovered that I had a unhealthy addiction to porn. As I grew into my teen years, I had girlfriends, but the only "sexual experience" I had was on the rare occasion when I was able to save up enough money and gumption to walk into a corner convenient store for a Playboy magazine. Fortunate for me, there was no internet.

As I grew into adulthood, I grew more fond of speaking on a stage. At the age of 14, I felt I was called to preach. I would preach on Sunday morning, having indulged in porn the night before. In my heart, I loved God and hated myself. I hated porn, but I couldn't stop looking at it. I began to experience long periods of depression. I eventually went on to become a youth minister and a pastor. With porn so scarce and getting caught a real possibility, I seldom bought it. Later, I would discover that this was a factor in causing my depression. With no porn, there was nothing available to meet that need. I was hooked on porn, and I didn't know how to turn to God's way of loving myself and others. The result? Depression.

Into my late 20's, I was able to keep my cycles of depression under wraps – except at home. It was when I was in my early 30's that my cycle got to be too much for my wife, Linda. It was late one evening – around 2 a.m. I believe – when I was in the depths of another bout of depression. Linda came to me and told me that if things didn't change that she was going to take our two children and leave me. You talk about a wake-up call. I told her that evening that I would get help, and the next day I did just that.

Pastor Frank of Second Avenue Baptist Church, in Bonneville, Maine, was a long distance mentor of mine. Frank had a retreat center at his church in Bonneville. I knew Frank had an annual pastors' conference at this church. I had always wanted to go. That next morning I called and discovered that the pastors' conference was the next week. I immediately made two reservations for Linda and me. I hustled home and told Linda the news. That next week, we drove to Maine and checked in. I couldn't believe my eyes when I looked at the program and read what the conference was about, "Overcoming Childhood Sexual Abuse."

Now, up until that time, I had not made the connection between my depression and the childhood abuse. However, I did find the title very intriguing. It definitely got my attention. You see, unlike what is portrayed in movies, one's childhood abuse isn't something you mysteriously don't remember and discover later. For people I have met, they not only remember it, their whole life is defined by it. Time came for the first session of the week to begin. Approximately 100 pastors and their wives were seated in the sanctuary. The speaker stood up to speak, and I could not believe what came out of his mouth.

That man stood up on a stage and began to recount how he was sexually abused as a child. I could not believe my ears! I can't believe how anyone could do this. I would never do that. As he talked, tears began to roll down my face. Linda looked over at me and asked what was wrong. I told her that the speaker was telling my story. Following the session, I walked right up to the speaker and told him about my abuse. I had never shared it with anyone. What a great week – but as the week was coming to an end, I began to get concerned. What do I do when I get home? I can't tell anyone I know about this. The speaker recommended Dr. Lacey. He had a counseling ministry based in Newton.

Little did I know that inner, spiritual *healing* was first going to be an inner, spiritual war. The war was to be fought between the lie – of who I had allowed the abuse to convince me I was—versus the me, Christ made me to be.

The Pathway to Healing

Once back home, I made an appointment to see Dr. Lacey. Little did I know, I would frequent his office often for the next four years. Looking back at the process, I can see ten steps to my healing.

Step one: Find a trusted friend, pastor, or counselor and tell them! I had to learn to trust Dr. Lacey. Something that the good doc said early on that has stayed with me to this day is, "God needs a face." I had never been in a close relationship with anyone! Especially when it comes to sharing the things I was going to have to reveal. This took a while. Learning to trust someone enough to risk opening wounds that scabbed over as long as mine had, was not easy – but once I let it out, the process to healing could begin.

Step two: Transparency. A principle I eventually learned is that secrecy is Satan's way of keeping us in prison to our past and pain. I had finally broken down and told Dr. Lacey everything, and I mean everything. Dr. Lacey asked, "Is that everything? Have you shared the absolute worst of all that happened to you and what you have done?" I answered, "Yes." Then he told me, "Corey, knowing the worst about you, I want you to know that I still love you and God does, too." I had never believed that I was loveable. Down deep, I believed that if you knew everything about me that you would not love me. You see, I believed I must have done something very bad to deserve this. You may say you love me, but if you knew the *real* me, you wouldn't – no way! That day, I discovered that when God says He loves us, He is not talking about when we are at our best. God loved me when I was at my worst. What a God!

Step three: Trust in God. I needed to let go and trust that God really can heal me. After I embraced the fact that God loved me no matter what, I quickly went on to trusting God with my life – even my hurts and pains.

Step four: I embraced my Identity in Christ. It is crucial that we believe what God says about us, not Satan's lies. I mentioned that the war was to be fought between the lie – of who I had allowed the abuse to convince me I was—versus the me, Christ made me to be.

Step five: Forgiveness. There is no healing without forgiveness. This required rewinding the video tape. When I became convinced I was who God made me to be, experiencing God's healing touch was just a "forgiveness" away. The instructions were simple. Me, the adult-Corey, went over, picked up the little boy-Corey in his arms, and hugged him. I told little-Corey that everything was going to be okay. I told him what a great kid he was and how God and I loved him. Dr. Lacey then told me to imagine Jesus in the room. Jesus, then appeared, hugging "us" until the little-Corey and I become one. Jesus, then went over, hugged Stan, and waved me over to them, and I hugged Stan, forgiving him.

Step six: Healing is about embracing everything God has made you to be at salvation. There are six miracles that happen at salvation. We must embrace these important realities if we are going to receive the healing we desire. At salvation:

1. We died. Colossians 3:3 "For you died and your life is now hidden with Christ in God."

2. We are made alive in Christ. Ephesians 2:4 "God, who is rich in mercy, made us alive with Christ."

3. We became a new person. 2 Corinthians 5:17 "If anyone is in Christ, he is a new creation. The old has gone, the new has come!"

4. We are completely forgiven. 2 Corinthians 2: 13-14 "He forgave us all our sins, having canceled the written code, with its regulations, that was against us and that stood opposed to us; he took it away, nailing it to the cross."

6. We have His life. Colossians 3: 3-4 "For you died and your life is now hidden with Christ in God. When Christ, who is your life, appears, then you appear with him in glory."

7. We are seated with Him in heaven. Ephesians 2: 4-10 "God raised us up with Christ and seated us with him in the heavenly realms with Christ."

One evening, while I was listening to Dr. Lacey preach, all these pieces came together. It was as though each principle was a different piece of a puzzle floating around in my mind. Everything came together. As I was sitting in my pew, a peace came over me that I just can't explain. Everything I was being taught for four years finally made sense. For the first time in my life, I actually embraced my identity in Christ! I was healed!

Step seven: Healing is being fully convinced that what God says about you is true. Spiritual or inner healing is both an event and a process – without a doubt, the event was the result of a process. Once healing takes place, the journey is really only beginning.

Step eight: A real part of your journey after healing is discovering "normal." Normal people have ups and downs. Normal people get depressed. Life doesn't always come with the exhilaration of the healing! There are two secrets to walking in newness of life – identity and purpose.

Step nine: People who have been abused as a child, usually have some sort of way they act out of dysfunction. For many it is homosexuality. For others, they develop some other sort of sexual dysfunction. For example, they go on to abuse others. For me, I became depressed and developed an unhealthy addiction to pornography. Ninety-nine point nine percent (99.9%) of the time this is no longer a problem for me. I have set parameters for myself. I have accountability partners and avoid the internet when I am alone. I wish I could announce to you that when I was healed that I was never tempted with porn again, but I cannot say that. As I mentioned above, for the majority of the time, porn does not even come to mind – it is not an issue. However, there are times when the temptation comes and it is difficult to overcome. The secret here is to remember that this isn't you and to immediately confess your sin and move on.

As you are reading this and if you have a problem with porn – you cannot overcome this by yourself. The first thing you need to do is to find a trusted friend or pastor and tell them! Again, secrecy is Satan's weapon to keep you in bondage. When you tell someone, you break his hold on you! The power over you is gone!

Step ten: Enjoy the journey. Enjoy life! When you embrace your identity in Christ and you are actively involved in God's purpose for your life – there is no greater place to be. At the time of this writing, I am over 20 years past my counseling and healing experience. Am I perfect? Far from it! There are times that I feel great and then there are times when life gets tough. As a general rule, I wake up each morning excited about the day. God has blessed me with a wonderful, loving wife and two adult children who are seeking after Him.

Corey

I pray that my story was a blessing to you. Remember, the journey begins by finding a trusted friend, pastor or counselor and telling somebody about your pain. My prayers are with you as you begin your journey!

Taken from the Bill Gaither song, *"He Touched Me"*:

Shackled by a heavy burden
'Neath a load of guilt and shame
Then the hand of Jesus touched me
And now I am no longer the same

Since the previous story is about an acquaintance, I see often, I can vouch for the reality of his testimony. He truly is a changed man.

CHAPTER 9
FORNICATION AND ADULTERY

A friend of mine made a remark that when "once seemingly sane people' are caught up in an adulterous sexual relationship they go crazy. In my experience as a counselor, I would say they become incapable of normal, rational reasoning. They become so self-centered that they could care less about how much they hurt other people. One of the most disturbing things I have to deal with, too often, is when a parent walks away from their children for another lover.

When I question them about hurting their children so deeply, I frequently get the same answer in the form of a question. What about ME? Don't I deserve to be happy? I explain to the adulterous parent that their betrayal and abandonment of their children will leave scars for life. Telling them that their happiness from immediate gratification will be short lived is like talking to a brick wall. God says, "The pleasures of sin are for a little season" translated (a very short time).

Hebrews 11:25.

Fornication and adultery are the two sexual sins referred to most often in the Bible. The word in the Greek for these two sins is porneia. The word encapsulates all sexual sins. When discovered, sexual sins are trust breakers. Unfortunately, in relationships trust is the most difficult problem to repair. It is impossible to have a good marriage without trust.

My brother Curt made this statement, and from my experience as a counselor, I agree. He said, "Sex outside of marriage is no Honeymoon." Jesus viewed adultery (the destroyer of marriage) as an issue so extreme that it is almost impossible to repair the marriage. The fact that adultery was the only sin Jesus allowed divorce and remarriage for is proof that adultery was not to be taken lightly. It must be understood, He only made this allowance for the innocent party. The guilty party will face God's consequence. It used to be 8.5 times out of 10 men were the instigators in fornication and adulterous relationships. Now I'm told that women today take the initiative just as often as men do.

Over the years, I have counseled with numerous clients who have told me they made a mistake and married the wrong person. It is always obvious they had a lot of anger resulting in withholding sexual intimacy. It is rare that both husband and wife agree that they made a mistake. The one who doesn't want out of the marriage is left with hurt and rejection.

In some cultures, marriages are arranged. They don't experience dating that leads to falling in love. I often wondered what percentage of those marriages go sour versus the way we do things in the Western culture. Also, who gets the blame when the marriage fails? Regardless of how or why people marry, the answer to a bad marriage is found in obedience to God. Interestingly enough, God didn't tell us to marry the person we fell in love with, He told us to love the person we are married to.

CHAPTER 10

RAPE

Date rape has been a problem for years. A very high percentage of young males just assume that sex is a part of dating. Because of this assumption, young men need to be taught and warned that taking advantage of girls on a date is not acceptable. There should be a penalty strong enough to be a deterrent. Boys should take full responsibility for their behavior. In addition, girls should also assume responsibility for their behavior. The parent(s) should teach their daughters what is appropriate dress and behavior while on a date. Girls who dress provocatively are asking for an inappropriate response from their date, which encourages irresponsible behavior leading to situations she may not be able to handle. In recent years, more and more females are taking the initiative, and then changing their minds after the guy forces himself on her.

Other rape situations more often than not are the result of a man who is angry toward females and forces himself on her as a way of punishing her. Both males and females are guilty of committing rape by taking advantage of vulnerable teenagers. Gang rape is physically and emotionally destructive to females. Often it causes a deep repressed anger that when exhibited is aimed at all males. For many it is almost impossible to experience a normal sexual intimacy in marriage.

During war times, military personnel on both sides often led by frustration and anger, commit rape of women and children in the war zone. Too often brutality is part of the act. Sometimes service-members rape fellow service-members. In some primitive uncivilized countries, sex is barbaric, cruel, and inhumane. Due to the lack of education, men do not show love and the women do not experience love and pleasure. In addition to teaching the people in uncivilized countries how to read, missionaries should also teach about and model what God's love looks like.

Washington State in their end of the year report regarding rape cases said that the lab that processes the rape kits is running 6,000 reports in arrears. And that figure does not include the most recent kits that have not been submitted for examination. The report showed that the number of reported rapes is up 86% over 2014. As the culture declines morally numbers of rape cases will increase.

In Idaho my home state there were 153 rape charges. Five were male rape cases. (Information provided by the Idaho Supreme Court)

Alexander Whyte, a prominent Englishman, wrote, "It was moral failure that has strewed the sands of time with the wreckage of civilization."

In response to a new report on numbers of rapes and other sexual assaults on high school and college campuses in the Coeur d'Alene Press in a weekly column it was reported, "It is important to create a culture which guides youth from an early age to see sex not as relationship entitlements." So far so good! "It is privilege; not as something to be had, but something to be given---and only if desired by both." Vice President Joe Biden in his remarks at the Oscars Academy Awards Night obviously like the press columnist recognized the urgency of dealing with sexual assaults on college campuses. Also, they both stated the importance of changing the culture. What they don't seem to understand is that mutual consent does not make the violation of the Creator's plan morally right, nor does it alleviate the consequences caused by violating God's plan for sex in traditional marriage. ONLY!

CHAPTER 11
SEX AND SUBSTANCE ABUSE

It is no secret that alcohol and drugs are adversarial components of hormones at parties. Every year thousands of teenagers lose their virginity on prom night or after graduation parties. Due to a diminished capacity to exercise control in logic, judgment, moral strength, and character when under the effects of alcohol or other mind-controlling substances, lives are often changed sexually forever. Some consequences are pregnancies, sexually transmitted diseases, guilt, anxiety, depression, lack of trust and an overall negative attitude toward sex.

Sometimes boys deliberately spike a girl's drink so that her ability to say NO is completely diminished. Bill Cosby is an example of this kind of perverted behavior. Frequently, rape is the result of alcohol and substance abuse. The act of partying that leads to sexual and perverted sexual activity is a huge problem among college students. Sometimes substance abuse and sexual activity are encouraged by professors. These kinds of problems are not limited to teenagers and college students.

Many adulterous relationships are the result of alcohol and other substance use. Extreme anger is often the result of adultery and broken trust, sometimes culminating in murder, especially when alcohol or drugs are involved. Some people argue that sex is more fulfilling when they are high on alcohol or drugs. However, there is enough evidence to prove that theory false.

Every year during Spring Break, thousands of college students go to Florida, Mexico, or the Caribbean to participate in what is considered part of the college experience. The parents of many of these students pay the costs of their college age kids to participate in this experience because they do not want their children to miss the making of memories. Some parents cough up the money because their sons and daughters put a guilt trip on them by saying all their friends are going.

The sad thing is these experiences and memories are not always positive. Alcohol is the drink of choice by most of the party revelers. Often drugs become part of the equation. Sexual inhibitions are blurred. Many young gals lose their virginity and some even get pregnant followed by abortions. Others acquire sexually transmitted diseases. Due to guilt and shame, these consequences are usually kept quiet. Sometimes this information is not shared with the students' parents.

Alcohol poisoning and drug overdose are not uncommon. For many, due to the mixture of alcohol, drugs, and sex (whether it is by choice, weakened inhibitions, or rape) their goals and plans for life are frequently altered forever.

One recent example is the notorious situation at a prominent university. Four young men brutally, sexually assaulted a female student after she got drunk and passed out. Two of the boys were star football players. They have been kicked off the team. All four of them have had to leave the University. They were tried in court and found guilty, and are waiting to be sentenced. Their lives along with the young lady have been changed forever.

CHAPTER 12
YOUTH AND SEXUAL CONFUSION

Other aspects of the college experience have to do with students who are trying to find their way in life. When I was doing campus ministry back in the 70's, a statement I heard frequently was, "I am trying to find myself." Back then, there were millions of students who felt lost and unfulfilled. It really isn't all that different today. Professors, psychologists, and counselors have not been very helpful. They encourage the students to experiment with their sexuality, etc. Another phrase during the 70's and 80's was, "just do your own thing." At a period in history when things were much like today in the Old Testament it said, "Every man did that which was right in his own eyes." Proverbs 21:2

Since sex is so prevalent on the college campuses, while trying to find their sexual identity, the students have become even more confused. The following are a few examples of the kinds of sexual events that are promoted at North Idaho College: Hallowqueen Drag Show celebrating gender and sexual identity as part of the Halloween festivities; another event presented by the Philosophy Club was titled "SEX What's It Good For."

It must be understood that I live in one of the most Conservative communities in one of the most Conservative states in the U.S. Having worked on numerous college campuses in more liberal communities, I know that the promotion of sexual perversion and promiscuity is much greater than here in North Idaho. I served on the North Idaho College Trustee Board for six years. I am a strong supporter of the college. There are some great people who serve in the administration, faculty, and staff.

43

There are some really good things about this Institution. However, for the benefit of the students, changes in the area of promoting immoral sexuality are necessary. While serving on the Board, I wrote the following letter to the editor of the Sentinel, the student newspaper, in response to a previously printed article brought to my attention by a student. Before passing this letter on to the readers of this book, I want to clarify a few things first. I want it to be understood that I was not speaking on behalf of the Trustee Board. Secondly, the Sentinel is not a publication of the college, it is a student designed and published newspaper. Finally, when I quoted Tony Stewart he was head of the Political Science Department. He has since retired. He is now the leading proponent of the same sex unions in our community.

Letter to the Sentinel

Sentinel Editor:

It has been brought to my attention several times during the past couple of years by students that there have been too many articles with too much graphic information on sex related topics in the Sentinel.

One student said she and some of her friends were embarrassed by the picture of condoms on the front page, the picture showing the placing of a condom on a banana and the picture of two guys in bed together is not acceptable on a community campus. A former student told me that handing out goody bags with condoms and lubricant during Safe Sex Week encourages more sex and is considered a big joke by many of the students.

Tony Stewart has said on several occasions, "If you have a great exchange of ideas, then each of us becomes better thinkers and doers."

Let me also add that the purpose of the exchange of ideas, scientific research, and sharing of philosophical differences should be the pursuit for and discovery of truth. With these thoughts in mind, I would like to share a few thoughts from a different perspective regarding the recent information shared on Sexual Awareness by Jay Friedman and Planned Parenthood.

First, let me preface my thoughts by saying as a member of Trustees of North Idaho College in conjunction with the other members of the Board, it is our responsibility to help provide for every student a quality education. Whether you are an academic major planning to further your education beyond NIC, a professional technical student, or work force trainee, it is my desire that you succeed in accomplishing your goals. I trust that my contribution along with the administration, faculty, and staff will play a significant role in your preparedness for life and future careers.

Secondly, I would like to share a few thoughts about sexuality based on my research and practice as a Family, Marriage, and Sexual Dysfunction counselor for more than 43 years. Differing perspectives on sexuality are the result of the lack of honest education, incorrect information, sexual abuse, especially at an early age, pornography, and perverted experimentation.

Last year Ann Trusdell made some valid points in her article. "College brings a whole new level to dating, heartbreak." She wrote about the simplicity of relationships in pre-high school and how that in high school when sex becomes an issue, things become even more complicated. She also wrote, "Then you get to college where everything is ambiguous. People have sex without being in a relationship, just for fun." These kinds of relationships cause distrust, jealousy, fear, anger, confusion, heartbreak, depression. loneliness, and guilt, often leading to suicidal thoughts, especially for girls.

Guys, let's accept responsibility for our actions and protect our female friends from all this emotional pain. Remember some day you will probably marry one of these damaged girls and you will both be less fulfilled sexually. Eschelle Lechot, in her column, "sex advice from a mom," in the article about threesomes, quoted "Dr. Gail Saltz, a psychiatrist, who appeared on a number of TV programs. She said, "If you bring a third party into the bedroom, it is impossible to prevent jealousy, embarrassment, possessiveness, and a slew of other emotions from creeping in. RETHINK IT! Before you do it!

To eliminate much of the confusion about sexuality, we must first determine who or what is the designer and Creator of sex. In other words, where did the idea of sex originate and what was its purpose? Either sexuality evolved or there was a mastermind who designed male and female, and created them to experience mutual fulfilment in marriage. If sexuality just evolved, who sets the parameters and makes the rules regarding sexual relations for physical, emotional, social, and spiritual well-being of society? To state it more clearly, whose morality do we embrace? Does each individual have the right to decide which set of morals is best for him or her? If sexuality is derived from the evolutionary process, is it still evolving and where can we expect it to go from here? As you can see from this line of thinking, and as Trusdell stated, things do get more complicated and confusing.

I choose to believe the Master–Designer theory that God, the Creator, created sex for a dual purpose – procreation and rec-creation. The Creator that knows how His creation works best gave us principles to govern our sexuality. His rules were given for our protection. As a matter of fact, He has our best interest in mind. He wants to save us from heartbreak. His plan calls for sexual intimacy only within the bonds of marriage. When His plan is followed, the physical and emotional problems related to sexually transmitted disease, AIDS, and unwanted pregnancy outside of marriage are virtually non-existent.

My research and experience as a counselor has shown that the Master-Designer Plan works best. His plan is superior because it almost eliminates anxiety, jealousy, possessiveness, guilt, and comparisons with other sexual partners. Also, sexual dysfunction is less prevalent because of the absence of guilt.

Let me conclude, by emphasizing one more time that I share these thoughts because I want you to enjoy and celebrate your sexuality to the fullest.

Ron Vieselmeyer

God's plan for man's (human) sexuality is always Best!!

While being interviewed on the O'Reilly Show in response to the huge increase in teachers having sex with their students, Andrea Tantaros said, "There are no boundaries any more. While they know it is wrong, and they know they will probably be caught, they don't seem to care anymore. We are an oversexed culture!"

CHAPTER 13
CELEBRITY SEX

Increasing numbers of celebrities and people in power are engaging in destructive adulterous relationships. These include entertainers, athletes, politicians, bosses, people in various positions of authority, etc. Some of these affairs result from people throwing themselves at celebrities. For some reason, they think that being intimately involved with a celebrity will make them special. Teenage girls work themselves into a frenzy and literally go crazy at rock concerts.

Many an affair is the result of famous, powerful people thinking they are entitled, and they can have whomever they want. While many of the affairs entertainers get involved in are destructive, there seems to be an attitude of "no big deal, everybody is doing it." The latest affair, breakup of a marriage, and new romances become part of the entertainment in celebrity magazines and prime time TV, Hollywood gossip shows, and soap operas.

Forty years ago, I did some counseling in Hollywood. I can tell you that new love affairs only bring a measure of fulfillment for most entertainers for a brief period of time. What is perceived to be the answer to emptiness in their lives, due to violating the Creator's plan for sexual fulfillment, only leaves them with empty feelings. While working in Hollywood, I asked numerous times the question of WHY? If fame and fortune were supposed to bring fulfillment, why are so many celebrities depressed, dependent on drugs, and are suicidal? Hollywood defies God in the personal lives of a high percentage of entertainers.

They glamorize immoral entertainment. The result leaves them with a heart-shaped vacuum.

I was personally involved in one situation where a life was totally destroyed because of a homosexual relationship with a world-renowned entertainer from whom he contracted AIDS. Famous people seem to have a way of making immoral deviant behavior more acceptable. Often when homosexuals are introduced or mentioned by name, it is usually followed by a title of gay or lesbian. Rosie O'Donnell, Ellen DeGeneres, and Elton John are examples of celebrity acceptance of immoral behavior. They have had Medals of Honor bestowed on them. For example, Elton John is not only adored by the masses, but the Queen of England knighted him. He is considered a role model the world over for his music and his immoral same sex union.

In the last 25 years there seems to be an epidemic of politicians being caught in a variety of sexual entanglements. We hear about deviant relationships of local elected officeholders, legislators, governors, U.S. Senators, Congressmen, even in the White House. Along with destruction of marriages and families, it also compromises elected officeholders ability to govern. Diplomacy prostitution has been used for centuries as a means to committing espionage. It is almost impossible to have violators of God's moral law removed from office.

These offenders show very little shame. The committing of sin doesn't seem to bother them. Their only disappointment is when they get caught. When confronted by the people who elected them as to their ability to perform their duties properly, they seem to think they can compartmentalize and keep their personal life separate from their public life. More and more Americans seem to be OK with their elected officials' immoral behavior. These officials don't seem to consider in advance the heartache they cause spouses and children because of their actions.

Having served in the Idaho Legislature, I personally know several elected officials who violated God's moral law. I counseled with and supported some of the Legislators and Congressmen through their painful experiences of guilt, rejection, and loss.

Some college and professional athletes seem to believe they are special, invincible, and above the team rules and the laws of society.

Due to the popularity of sports stars, people who are attracted to fame and money make themselves available to the athlete. These kinds of encounters can be nothing more than a one-night stand or it could lead to a friendship. More often than not, it turns out to be a very short-term ego booster for both parties. Too often, these ego boosts end in heartbreak.

Naïve vulnerable young people quickly latch onto these famous people. They develop a romantic attachment to their hero. Sometimes they fantasize a romantic attachment long before meeting their hero. While they fall hard, the athletic hero usually has nothing more in mind than to respond to the demands of his hormones. Many of these athletes have had sexual encounters with hundreds, in some cases more than 1000 women.

Women seem easily attracted to men in leadership or authority. In turn, many a boss has taken advantage of these vulnerable women. Sometimes the employer takes advantage of the employee, especially if they are aware of the employee having marital problems. Sometimes it is the reverse; the employer is the one having marital problems.

CHAPTER 14
FAILURES OF THE CLERGY

A major frustration for me as a counselor and a minister is working with clergy who have violated their own consciences. I have worked with several ministers who have gotten involved in different kinds of deviant sexual relationships. Ninety percent of these infidelities started with pornography and in most cases, it led to addictions. Pornography leads to curiosity, which leads to acting it out. In most cases, the priests and ministers who have practiced immoral behavior are disappointed in themselves and become ineffective in their ministries.

Four minsters with whom I counseled had arrogant attitudes, and when I suggested they step aside from the ministry, they dug in their heels and refused to resign. My disappointment is that these religious leaders are supposed to be the leading moral compass to the community. They refused in their personal lives to practice the principles that God has given us to live by, notably self-discipline. Hypocritical is the best way to describe these religious leaders who put on a pious front when behind the pulpit or in the confessional booth, contrary to who they were behind closed doors.

The numbers of religious leaders who have committed sins of unfaithfulness are unknown. However, many lives have been impacted by their behavior. Entire congregations and communities experience hurt, disappointment, and shame. Tragic can't fully describe the emotional, moral, social, and spiritual harm that is perpetrated on marriages, families, and children who have been molested. Some homosexual ministers and priests twist the truth of God's Word in defiance to defend their immoral behavior. Since these so-called moral leaders in society distort the truth, it causes ambivalence and confusion for those who are seeking hope and truth. God says these leaders, who know the truth, have a greater responsibility. Therefore, the consequences are greater.

While some members of the clergy have perverted their personal lives, damaged the lives of those whom they have abused, and embarrassed their congregations, some have committed an even greater harm.

Webster's definition of harm: Moral Injury; evil, wrong. They have taken the lead in promoting immorality (same sex unions) to their congregations causing major divisions in the local church and/or denomination.

Webster's definition of perversion: Any of various sexual practices that are commonly regarded as being abnormal. Pervert: To lead astray morally; to turn away from the right course. Typically, clergy (moral and theological leaders of the church and community) are well versed in spiritual discipline. One of Webster's definitions of discipline: The system of government regulating the practice of a church or order.

Romans 1:28 says that those who are practicing gays and lesbians, even though they are knowledgeable… "they did not like to retain God in their knowledge, therefore God gave them over to a morally depraved mind."

Another way ministers fail their congregations and society is by their refusal or inability to take a public stand against sexual immorality, especially homosexuality. Some ministers have a fear of losing church members and/or their 501(c) 3 exemptions. Others just do not want to get involved in an issue that is controversial.

When our local city council passed the same sex ordinance, two ordained ministers (who ran a wedding chapel) were caught in the middle of the controversy. The local media and the NBC affiliate in Spokane, WA contacted several local ministers to get some feedback about this controversial topic. The media reporter told me most of the ministers refused to comment. Six of them said they would call back, but never did. This resulted in my being the only religious leader being interviewed. Some of the ministers referred the reporters to me.

Many a well-meaning minister gives female members of his congregation a hug regularly. Unfortunately, we live at a time when large numbers of women have been abused earlier in life, and they just cringe at the thought of being hugged by a man. Some have left the church over this issue. A much higher percentage of women are desperate for affection. They look forward to their weekly hug from the pastor. In cases where the woman is single or is having problems in her marriage, she may read more into the hug than the weekly greeting. In addition, sometimes the reverse happens if the minister is having problems in his marriage.

I share these thoughts not to condemn, but to help you see things more clearly from a counselor's perspective, as shared with me by numerous clients over the years. Also, for the sake of the Gospel, and the healing of deep emotional wounds, I encourage you to be discreet.

Since it is expected that we, the clergy, should be the moral leaders in the community I am asking you to join me by taking a stand in the public arena for absolute moral TRUTHS.

CHAPTER 15
SEX SLAVE TRADE

Recently, my wife and I spent some time visiting orphanages in Third World Countries where children have been rescued from the sex slave trade. We spoke to some of the rescuers. While we have limited knowledge of the impact of the perverted offenses perpetrated on these children, we have a better understanding. Primarily, being taken from one's parents, siblings, and familiar secure surroundings is devastating. I cannot imagine the fear experienced by these children when they are first kidnapped, sold into slavery, and then forced to endure gruesome perverted sex with numerous adults every day. One person who works with these children told us their minds are so polluted that they can never think normally about their sexuality or experience a normal sex life. Often the victims grow up to be offenders.

There are upwards of two million children who are involved in the sex slave trade, and more than 50,000 women and children are smuggled into the United States as sex slaves annually. There is no punishment harsh enough for the offenders of these children. Jesus said, "A millstone should be hung around their necks and they should be thrown into the water and drowned."

Apart from the sex trade, there are millions of other children who are sexually abused by adults. There are numerous cases where a woman, a teenager, or a child is enslaved by one man or a small group of men and women. This kind of abuse perpetrated on these captives is horrific, unbelievable brutality. It is almost like a plague except the adults who practice this deviant behavior are making conscious evil choices. The selling and trading of innocent children for the sexual gratification of evil men and women is atrocious beneath human dignity. Webster's definition of atrocious: extremely or shockingly wicked; cruel or brutal, abominable.

It is inconceivable but in some cases, these children are sold into captivity by their parents. However, more often these kids are kidnapped. These children are desperately waiting to be rescued. Once they are rescued, they have a difficult time adjusting to normal life. They have been deprived of normal teaching and modeling. It is impossible for them to free their minds from the perverted acts that have been forced upon them. It takes counseling and a miracle for them to live a semblance of a normal life.

I think we can all agree that kidnapping and selling children in the sex trade is horrendous. The perpetrators should be prosecuted to the full extent of the law. Interestingly enough, the most hated inmates in our jails and prisons are those who have committed crimes against children. Isn't it just as horrendous to dismember an innocent baby in the womb or by murdering the baby by partial birth abortion? Isn't it an offense to children who are taught by a parent or a teacher that unnatural, immoral sex is normal, thus confusing their thinking and causing them to question their sexuality?

CHAPTER 16
VULGARITY AND PROFANITY

<u>Vulgarity and Profanity</u>: Unless one is deaf, I do not need to tell you about the prevalence of vulgarity and profanity. We hear it quite regularly from some individuals or groups of people, such as construction workers. Children are told it is not nice to use certain words. They grow up with the idea that those are adult words. Just like with smoking and drinking alcohol, when parents model this type of behavior, the children can't wait until they are old enough to use those vulgar words too. In some cases, parents or other adults teach children vulgarity because they think it is cute.

Some members of society try to impress us by how mature they are by how often they use the F word, etc. If you pay close attention to how these people act, they really are quite immature. These immature people spend much of their time sharing off-color stories and jokes. For those who are close to those telling obscene jokes, but choose not to participate, they are made to feel like prudes or goody-goodies.

I don't need to spend more time on this segment of the subject other than to ask why is there such a tremendous amount of vulgarity spoken about sexual activity or sexual parts of the anatomy. It is just another way that man shows disdain and hatred for what God intended to be beautiful. The use of profanity is mockery of the Creator.

People of all ages are participating in immature displaying of their privates on the Internet. Unfortunately, children and teenagers are losing the mystique of innocence, which can never be retrieved. They will never again have the experience of solemnly standing before God, family, and friends pure and guilt free on their wedding day.

CHAPTER 17

SWINGING

<u>Swinging</u>: Swinging is when couples exchange partners for sexual experiences. Sometimes it is by couples who know each other. Sometimes it is with people they have met on the internet for a one-time tryst. Sometimes it occurs through parties, hot tubbing, and clubs and bars with numerous couples participating. These swinging encounters always cause jealousy and broken trust between husband and wife. I know of one situation where the jealousy led to murder. Regarding the trust factor, it is impossible to have a good marriage without trust. The result of swinging is a very high percentage of the couples who participate in this end up divorced.

People of all ages and levels of the social ladder suffer from the pain of broken marriages. It has a snowballing effect that impacts people far beyond the immediate husband and wife. The children in particular and other members of the family and friends also suffer.

Periodically a couple will admit this kind of behavior is demeaning. They come for counseling with a desire to make the marriage work. The problem is they can't remove all the other sexual experiences from their mind. This results in comparisons, jealousy, and lack of trust. These kinds of practices have a way of desensitizing shame, thereby destroying the sacredness and oneness of intimacy.

A former client talked his wife into accompanying him on a visit to an adult sex store, where she learned about a variety of sexual practices. Her husband then wanted her to experiment in perverted behavior including participating in wife swapping. The thought of participating in this kind of behavior made her feel dirty, angry, guilty, and sick to her stomach. Most importantly, the fact that he tried to persuade her to participate in wife swapping, just once, destroyed her trust and respect for him. It also ruined their marital intimacy. Their marriage ended in divorce, and her husband ended up in the State Penitentiary for molesting a child. These kinds of situations happen all too often. One deviant behavior can open doorways to more.

CHAPTER 18
INCEST AND POLYGAMY

Incest: I have written about a number of deviant sexual behaviors, including problems and consequences. Of all the different sexual practices, incest is one of the most secretive. In my counseling, I have dealt with a variety of incestual relationships. For example, father with daughter, mother with son, brother with sister, brother-in-law with sister-in-law, aunts, uncles, and cousins, etc. The most prevalent is stepfather with stepdaughter. This all too often is a consequence of broken families, which leads to step-families, blended families, and foster homes.

There are many sexually abused kids in foster homes who live with fear, anxiety, shame, guilt, depression, suicidal thoughts and attempts. Fear and shame cause members of the family who are aware of the incest, even if they are not participating, to hide knowledge of this deviant behavior. Sometimes they cannot believe this kind of behavior is happening in their home. Rather than report the crime, they go into a state of denial. Often times it is important for them to protect their family, friends, and neighbors. The main consequences of this decadent behavior are repressed anger and broken trust. Other consequences of incest are unwanted pregnancies, abortions, sexually transmitted diseases, and confusion regarding love and normal fulfilling sexual experiences.

The following story is that of a lady in her mid-seventies who struggled with normalcy most of her life.

Gigi's Story

I was the only girl in my family with four boys. My dad was an alcoholic. My mom was co-dependent. That was in the 1940's. Many men drank, but alcoholism was not talked about. I was 13 years old when the Mayo Clinic diagnosed my dad. He was such a nice man when he was not drinking, but when he drank, he was angry and mean. My mother would come to my bedroom to get away from him. She knew how much I meant to my dad so he did not bother us there, but I did not get any sleep because I was already upset with hearing them argue and fight. Consequently, I failed the fourth grade. That is when my mother started paying attention. She started working with me using flashcards in math and spelling. She was proud of me then. I did well with my studies.

My dad was sexual with me as a little girl (is it any wonder I learned not to trust men at an early age). Dad would bring his drinking buddies over when mother was at a bridge club. He would tell us, "Go upstairs, take off your clothes and lay on the bed." (He was showing off his kids, must have looked cute.)

Our ages at that time were 7, 5, 4, and 3. They would come to the door smiling and grinning. I knew what my Dad was going to do. How did I know? I was only five at the time. A therapist gave me the answer. He had done it before.

My dad used to call me "Scatterbrain." Of course I was. I was abused continually. I had been hurt, not been allowed to develop normally. I have wondered what happened to me, why I was in a fog, and that was it; abuse underachieving because of abuse, and more verbal abuse for not living up to their standards. More abuse because my brothers heard me so they abused me. My mom and dad did not come to my rescue- But GOD did!

Because of what my Dad did, I did not feel loved by him. I craved love from a man, but was confused as the men in my life made me feel that having sex was love. It took a long time to understand that love and sex were not the same thing. I now know that sex is an expression of love in marriage.

Gigi

Polygamy is a practice by sex-crazed men who do not want to commit adultery but are not satisfied with one woman. Usually they live in a commune. Like so many religious extremists, they brainwash and control their followers into believing their perverted lifestyle is supported by God's principles. They know that indoctrinating their children from an early age, both by teaching and modeling, that children accept their teachings as truth.

There are a number of moral and social problems related to these deviant practices. The young girls are pressured into marrying at an early age. Often, they end up marrying a much older man because they were persuaded to believe it was God's will, so they surrender to his will. In the polygamous family, a wife does not have a full-time husband, and children never have a full-time father.

Since the children don't know anything different, they assume what they have been taught is the truth. Sometimes one or two of the young girls run away from the commune. This creates another set of problems. Once they leave, they have no extended family. They live with a considerable amount of guilt. In addition, it is very difficult to adapt to the real world. Once again, this is the result of man rejecting God's plan and in the process destroying peoples' lives.

CHAPTER 19
SUICIDE

Suicide: Suicide is the intentional taking of one's own life; sometimes referred to as self-murder. The following are some of the reasons people commit suicide as related to sexual sins. Sex triangles that lead to painful rejection, shame, not wanting to face family or friends after being found out about one's adultery; not being able to live with the guilt, anxiety, and depressions that always accompany one's sins; not being able to face the possibility of facing prison time; (the consequential probability) for rape, incest, pedophilia, etc., drives the offender to take his or her life.

Sometimes the victim will take his or her life due to pseudo guilt, shame, hate, anger, and loss of self-worth. These factors can cause the victim to lose their desire to live.

Just as in the case of murder, there seems to be no limit to the astronomical numbers of lives that have been impacted. More often than not, people find it harder to accept a suicide than a murder. Family, friends, and society as a whole feel guilt and ask WHY? What could I have done differently is a question that leads to shame often followed by blame. In most cases, the guilt continues to haunt family and close friends the rest of their lives. Approximately, one-third of teenage homosexuals attempt suicide.

CHAPTER 20

MURDER

<u>Murder</u>: Often pedophilia and murder go together. If the pedophile feels he cannot trust the child following insidious behavior, they will murder the child and hide or destroy the body in order to cover up the evidence. Sometimes a pedophile will murder a child as part of a perverted sexual ritual. Investigators and law enforcement do not know how many missing persons, especially children, have been sexually tortured and murdered.

Murder as it relates to the subject of this book is the result of excessively strong sexual desires for a person other than one's own spouse. These love triangles periodically end with one party committing murder. The purpose of murder is to remove the person who stands in the way of a coveted romance.

I lived in Ontario, Canada for eleven years not far from the area where Russell Williams tortured and murdered two women. Russell was base commander and one of the highest-ranking officers in the Canadian Air Force. He got involved in pornography. Eventually, his curiosity drove him to breaking into homes where he stole women's lingerie. That led him to a deviant lifestyle of acting out by taking pictures of himself wearing the stolen underwear. One act led to another until he became a perverted sexual addict. He could not control his addiction, but became very good at living a double life. He did an outstanding job of performing his duties in the military. When Queen Elizabeth came to Canada, he was asked to be the pilot to fly her around the country. His addiction led to experimenting with all kinds of sexual acts including rape, torture, and eventually to the murdering of two women in an attempt to cover up sexual crimes. Russell Williams is now serving a life sentence in a Canadian penitentiary.

Most of us would probably say how could anyone commit such heinous crimes? I could never do that! However, fifty plus years ago I heard Ken Opperman, a minister in Toronto, preach on the subject of sin. During his sermon he said, "There is not one of us who is not capable of committing any sin in the book." He paused for a moment, a hush fell over the audience, and then he raised his voice, pointed his finger randomly toward the audience as he with a booming voice repeated himself, "There is not one of us who is not capable of committing any sin given the right set of circumstances." He paused again, raised his voice one more time, again saying, "I said GIVEN THE RIGHT SET OF CIRCUMSTANCES." He then lowered his voice and stated, "You are responsible for the circumstances." He then quoted the text that tells us we are to flee from temptation. I have never forgotten that brief challenge that morning. It definitely had an impact on my life knowing that if I had not learned that lesson I could be just as vulnerable to commit any sin in the book as Russell Williams.

The following text can be helpful in our efforts to avoid sinful circumstances. Philippians 4:8 "Whatever is true, whatever is honorable, whatever is just, whatever is pure, whatever is lovely, whatever is commendable THINK about these things." I do not know the percentage of murders committed due to jealousy, hatred, love triangles, etc., versus murders committed during robberies, uncontrolled anger, etc. From the stories, we hear in the news and documentaries, the numbers of murders due to relationships gone sour are very high.

The sad thing is that Hollywood in its movies and sitcoms glamorize these stories of heartache for entertainment purposes. The consequences of murder go way beyond just taking a life. Broken trust, broken lives, heartache, rejection, sorrow, anger, guilt, shame, depression, and anxiety are just some of the consequences. Murder destroys families, marriages, and lives of children. Children's lives are not only ruined by the loss of a parent or stepparent, but also guilt, as often they blame themselves for whatever went wrong that led up to the murder. Children are often put into a situation where they don't know who to believe. Sometimes they feel forced to take sides. Then there are times when the children are placed in a home of another family member or even in a completely unfamiliar home because of it.

The remaining spouse, co-conspirator in a murder situation have their own set of consequences relating to families, being ostracized, court hearings, paying attorneys, jail time, including most of the above listed consequences. It is like throwing a stone in the lake, the rippling effect just keeps going. It not only impacts the people that are directly involved, but friends, families, neighbors, communities, the culture, law enforcement, medical and psychiatric costs. Ultimately, you and I are impacted monetarily through paying higher taxes.

If we add the approximately 57 million abortions in America to the total of other sex related murders, more lives are taken from sex related murders than any other cause.

CHAPTER 21
LUST AND VOYEURISM

Lust and Voyeurism are basically sexual sins of the mind. *The definition of Lust: Intense, uncontrolled sexual desire.* Everyone more than likely commits sexual lust sooner or later. We have no way of measuring the numbers of people or the number of times people commit the sin of lust.

Humans can be secretive and deceptive with other humans. Only God knows the truth, and He makes it clear that if we lust we are guilty of adultery, Matthew 5:28. Therefore, there is nobody who has never committed a sexual sin.

Definition of Voyeurism: A person who obtains sexual gratification by looking at sexual objects and or acts. Voyeurism is a close relative to lust. They often go hand in hand secretively. Whether the reason for perverted thoughts is pornography, lust or voyeurism, Proverbs 23:9 says, "As a man thinketh in his heart so is he." Therefore, it is our responsibility to focus our minds on those things that are pure and honest.

CHAPTER 22

TRANSSEXUAL, BISEXUAL, CROSSDRESSERS

People who call themselves transsexual, bisexual, or cross-dressers are becoming more bold and are creating new problems that demand a solution such as which public restroom they should use. Liberal attorneys and judges are having a heyday supporting abnormal behavior and forcing their deviant solutions to the problems upon those who are normal.

While writing this sequel on perverted sexual behavior, I turned on the news. The headline was about which public restroom should be used by transgender, crossdressers, bisexuals, lesbians, and homosexuals in one public school district in California. The response to the question by a psychologist was- if you feel like a female, use the girls' restroom. If you feel like a male, use the boys' restroom. To make sure all bases are covered, urinals should be placed in all restrooms.

If this line of reasoning were not so pathetic, it would be funny. This problem could be resolved, but sometimes it takes a little sarcasm to get a point across. The schools could place a number of Port-a-Potties in the hallways with sex orientation and gender identification labels on the doors such as crossdressers, transgender, bisexual, lesbians, and homosexuals. Sometimes the only way you can get the attention of the absurd is by using absurdity.

I thought I had covered most of the bases in regards to sexual perversions. Then the President of the United States, with the support of the ACLU spoke out in support of public schools responsibility to provide privacy restrooms for students of all deviate sexual behaviors.

In his first term, President Obama signed hate crime legislation that became the first federal civil rights protection for transgender people in U.S. history. Since then, the Administration has quietly applied the power of the Executive branch to obtain health insurance under the Affordable Care Act. He ordered treatment for veterans for medical problems related to deviant sexual behavior at Veterans Administration facilities. The government contracted health insurers to start covering the cost of gender reassignment surgeries. A decade old rule preventing Medicare from financing such procedures was overturned within the Department of Health and Human Services. This was part of the news article titled, "Without Fanfare, Obama Advances Transgender Rights."

Bruce Jenner is the most recent celebrity to go public about his gender change. He is getting more attention for his new identity than he got for his Olympic stardom in the decathlon. If you don't accept the new "she" as being normal, you are not compassionate.

It never ceases to amaze me the extremes liberals will go to to destroy that which is good. The American Civil Liberties Union is threatening the autonomy of the local school districts in Idaho. They say the dress code is unconstitutional because it discriminates by gender.

Cassia County School District requires all female students participating in the graduation to wear white or pastel colored dresses.

Male graduating students must wear pants and a tie. The ACLU legal director Richard Eppink said, "Schools that make a distinction between boy and girl dress codes are enforcing gender stereotyping policies which violate state and United States Constitutions."

The next thing you know the ACLU will visit your homes to make sure your attire doesn't violate our Constitutions.

Is there any such thing as reason, logic, and commonsense? How did we survive before the age of the ACLU?

Most Idahoans will support the Cassia County dress code.

Therefore, I trust you will not cave in to the ACLU.

CHAPTER 23

SADOMASOCHISM

<u>Sadomasochism</u>: The following is limited information about degrading sexual practices by people who have rejected their Creator's plan but are desperately trying to find fulfillment. The repulsive practices of sadism, masochism, and sadomasochism are more common than most of us would like to believe.

<u>Definitions</u>:

Sadism: *Inflicting pain on others.*

Masochism: *Inflicting pain on one's self or receiving the infliction of pain from another person.*

Sadomasochism: *Sexual gratification gained through inflicting or receiving pain.*

A few of the degrading sexual practices associated with the above definitions are self-denial, submissiveness, whipping, bondage, etc., with the intent of experiencing pleasure through bizarre rituals. These kinds of perverted sexual practices are harmful to the body and psyche. Ultimately, they are extremely destructive spiritually and socially.

CHAPTER 24
FEMALE CIRCUMCISION

Strange barbaric sexual practices still exist in some Third World countries. The people are trapped in the traditions of the Dark Ages. Female circumcision, sometimes referred to as genital mutilation, is one of those traditions. It involves removing the clitoris from the female anatomy by using a sharp object such as a sharp stone.

In ages past, jealous husbands performed this surgical act on their wives so they could not enjoy sexual intimacy. His reasoning for doing this was to prevent her from having an affair. This practice eventually developed into a tradition with the mother or grandmother performing the surgical act on the young daughters or granddaughters. In this enlightened age, they are still doing this to young girls just because it was done to them.

This is another example of the kind of bizarre behavior practiced by human beings when they reject God's plan.

CHAPTER 25
BESTIALITY

Bestiality, along with incest, is also a perverted practice that is kept secret. It is best described as self-indulgent, filthy debauchery.

My informal research tells me it is more prevalent than we would like to believe. I will not graphically describe this behavior other than to say it is sickeningly repulsive.

CHAPTER 26
PROSTITUTION

In the Gospels, we read that the love of money is the root of all evil. Frankly, it means that people will do just about anything to get money, including the selling of their bodies. A client told me her husband had previously been a male-prostitute. In my experience counseling with prostitutes, both male and female, I learned that most of them had had sex with multitudes of people. This behavior destroys their ability to commit themselves to one person in a marriage. I interviewed several prostitutes. All but one of them told me they hated what they were doing but did not know what else to do to make a living. They hated themselves because they were living a lie to their families.

They also lived in fear of some clients, their pimps, and contracting sexually transmitted diseases. They had to be checked regularly for diseases. They all admitted to suffering from depression and anxiety. One gal had an arrogant attitude. She bragged about making more money than her family and friends could make at a legitimate job. She said she was not willing to give up her six figure income. She did admit that she would have to give up prostituting in a few years as eventually she would not be able to compete with younger women. She told me her daughter believed she was waiting tables at a high-end restaurant.

I spoke with a pimp (he called himself an agent). He told me that in some cities there are more male prostitutes than female prostitutes. One thing became very obvious to me while talking with people in the trade: there is a lot of jealousy among both male and female prostitutes. As you can see, the life of a prostitute is confusing, complicated, and dangerous. It is a very risky business. Sometimes young teenage girls are beaten into submission by their pimps. The result is they are afraid to try to escape.

In most states, prostitution is illegal. However, there are places where the selling of one's body for money is legal, as long as government regulations and local ordinances are met. Legal or illegal, prostitution is immoral.

North Idaho, where I live, has a history of prostitution. In its heyday mining towns, especially in the area called the Silver Valley, prostitution was practiced openly. Brothels (often referred to as whore houses, sometimes called houses of ill repute or comfort stations,) were often located in the center of the mining towns.

Today, prostitutes claim they provide a valuable service. However, in most places the so-called provision of service is more subtle. While it is impossible to estimate how many people visit brothels, I am sure the numbers are much higher than most of us would guess.

As a counselor, the kinds of people I see periodically who visit prostitutes regularly are long haul truck drivers and businessmen who travel a great deal. With many of these people the excitement of new experiences has become an addiction, so much so this behavior has been referred to as an epidemic.

There are numerous consequential complications such as sexually transmitted diseases, fear, guilt anxiety, and depression both for prostitutes and those who frequent their place of business, hotel rooms, etc. In cases when a spouse, other members of the family, or friends, finds out you have a whole new set of problems: broken marriages, broken families, and lack of trust.

A client of mine, who traveled extensively, got caught up in this lifestyle as he called it. It became an addiction. It had such a strong grip on him that everything he tried to free himself ended in failure. He said he still loved his wife, but because of his guilt he could not give himself totally to her. He became suicidal. His wife knew something was wrong but could not figure it out. She questioned him in regard to what might be causing the anxiety and depression. He did not only tell her one lie after another, he was living a lie.

A relative of his accidentally found out about one of his encounters and confronted him. He agreed to seek help and came to me for counseling. Eventually, he told his wife. She was very angry and started to make plans to leave him. But she agreed to give him a second chance. After more than a year of counseling, both of them worked through a lot of distrust. They now have a stronger marriage than they ever had before.

While this situation, after a lot of heartache, has worked out for the good of the whole family, more often than not, the outcome is disastrous.

Prostitution in countries where we have service-men stationed is huge business. The impact on military personnel is enormous. While part of God's plan for sex is Rec Creational, He did not intend for it to be rec-creational outside of marriage. When our servicemen have sex with multiple partners there are consequences such as the possibility of acquiring sexually transmitted diseases, guilt and problems related to comparisons of sex partners. These issues often have an ongoing impact in marriage.

Prostitution, along with other immoral sex practices, have a way of making inroads into our military, playing a major role in lowering the morale of many of our servicemen and servicewomen.

Also, while it is impossible to determine the real cost of this behavior both for our servicemen, the American culture, and the societies where our servicemen are stationed, we can be assured the cost is astronomical.

An atrocity of the Korean War was the Japanese forcing thousands of Asian women into prostitution. Historians say upwards of 200,000 Asian women were forced to provide sex to Japanese soldiers. These women were called "comfort women."

ISIS has been very good at keeping their atrocities under wraps. Recently, little by little, information has been coming to the surface about atrocious behaviors by radical Islamists. Women and children as young as five years of age are forced to serve in brothels. Angelina Jolie, in her preview of the movie Unbroken, made reference to sexual violence in time of war. She said, "It is time to put a stop to this kind of brutal behavior."

Prostitution resulting from the sex slave trade is the second most lucrative industry in the world. It has been predicted that human sex trafficking will soon surpass drug trafficking as the most prolific. The sex slave trade of innocent children is atrocious and beneath human dignity. Only a very small percentage of these children held in captivity are able to break free from their captors.

The following is a story from one of my clients:

Danny's Story

I have been married for 25 years to a wonderful Christian wife with many happy memories. Earlier in my marriage, I was very frustrated and went outside my marriage to a prostitute, which I really regretted. I confessed to my wife and because of her strong faith, she forgave me, which at the time I thought was a miracle.

Danny

We must remember that those who utilize the services of prostitutes are just as guilty of violating God's plan as those who are selling their bodies.

Let me plead with you whether you are a provider or a recipient of these services, PLEASE flee temptation and seek help.

CHAPTER 27

TEMPLE PROSTITUTION

Temple prostitution is another form of perverted sexual practices. It is somewhat akin to both prostitution and witchcraft. This heinous practice was a mix of religion and physical sexual gratification. In the Old Testament, this distortion of what was supposed to be spiritual worship to God turned into a mix of sexual ritual and idol worship. Worship accompanied by sexual orgies was like mockery and spitting in the face of God. Both females and males did not only sell their bodies to people with sex addictions, but to satan himself.

Along with homosexuality and sexual abuse of children, this practice was one of the most grievous sins against a Holy God.

CHAPTER 28
WITCHCRAFT

All around the world groups of people get together to practice satan worship often combined with debased torturous sexual practices. The question often asked is WHY? The answer is when people reject God's beautiful plan those with the most perverted minds turn to witchcraft or Satanism and practice sickeningly ugly orgies. They hand over the control of their lives and became slaves to that which is evil. They cannot decipher between right and wrong morally, socially, and spiritually. All too often, they end up having major mental problems.

From time to time, I have had clients who broke free from the enslavement of satan worship. However, most of them continue to have major mental and emotional problems such as extreme anxiety, panic attacks, and depression.

CHAPTER 29

NEW TRENDS

When we violate God's plan regarding marital intimacy we cease to be at peace with ourselves and with our Creator. The result is sexual thoughts have a way of taking control of our mind. They occupy a much greater percentage of our thought life. This in turn drives us to act on our thoughts culminating in experimentation with all kinds of deviant sexual activity.

The following are a few of the new trends in mankind's desperation to find sexual fulfillment. Some people make connections via the smartphone for one purpose only, to have sex. There is no communication other than that which is directly related to sex. When they have completed the engagement, they say good-bye and go their separate ways without knowing anything else about the other person with whom they were just sexually intimate. One man said he utilizes this service when he is home alone at night and gets bored.

Then there are those who prefer being a bit more social so they put a picture of themselves on the screen along with a one to three word statement of their interests such as skiing or Italian gourmet dining. Still others have dating encounters where it is understood that sex is not expected. However, if both agree after a dinner date, it is OK to have sex.

When being asked how often and how many times they engage in these new trend activities, the responses varied anywhere from once a month to five times a day. People who participate in these activities have had encounters as few as a dozen times and some more than 100 times.

Is it any wonder sexually transmitted diseases are becoming more rampant!!Sexting and sextortion are becoming popular ways of sexual interaction. People of all ages are participating in immature displaying of their privates. Unfortunately, children and teenagers are losing the mystique of innocence that can never be retrieved. They will never again have the experience of solemnly before God, family, and friends to be pure and guilt free on their wedding day.

To put it simply: sexting and sextortion are becoming popular ways of causing arousal and curiosity that, in turn, leads to unnatural sexual behaviors.

CHAPTER 30

FIFTY SHADES OF GREY VERSUS ONE SHADE OF WHITE

The making of the movie "Fifty Shades of Grey" is at the forefront of Hollywood's most recent controversial attempt at off-color entertainment. I have not read this book, and I have no intention of reading it or seeing the movie. From what I have heard about the reviews and have been told by a couple of friends, this film is not wholesome entertainment. It is the promotion of a deviant lifestyle. To view the trailer, one must be aware that the story is erotic fiction, and when signing in, you must include your age. One person who writes reviews said he doesn't usually write negative ones. He said he usually lets people decide for themselves, but in this case, he would not recommend this movie.

Idaho State law prohibits places that are licensed to serve alcohol from showing movies that depict sexual acts. The film in question that brought this issue to the attention of the Idaho State Police and the Courts is "Fifty Shades of Grey" being shown at the Village Cinema which has a liquor license.

The viewing of and practicing of sinful behavior is pleasurable. However, after reading what God has to say and from experience as a counselor, this kind of pleasure is very short lived. The Bible says, "the pleasures of sin are for a little season." I suggest you avoid immoral behavior because too often it leads to sexual addiction.

Isaiah 1:18 says, "Though your sins be as scarlet they shall be as white as snow. Though they be red like crimson, they shall be as wool."

The purity of white overshadows all 50 shades of grey. For the sake of making a point for the moment, let us substitute one shade of red or scarlet for 50 shades of grey.

The message being if we confess our sins and repent, God will forgive us of those destructive sins that stand out like a sore thumb. He will make us pure and clean as depicted by the whiteness of snow and wool. God also tells us if we acknowledge and denounce our sins, He will remove them as far as the East is from the West. He will bury them in the bottom of the deepest sea and He will forget all about them forever.

CHAPTER 31
DECEIT AND DISTRUST

In summing up this chapter, I think of it as being the variety or miscellaneous chapter. Typically, when a number of issues are listed as miscellaneous, they don't stand alone, therefore, they are considered minor issues. Not in this case! This portion of the chapter is about dishonesty. When people are caught up in practicing immoral behavior, they automatically become defensive and lie about their immorality. He or she usually lies repeatedly to cover up the first lie. Lying and distrust go hand in hand. Sometimes planned murder is the choice of action for trying to cover up one's sexual sins.

It has been said that people with addictions are masters of deception. Usually they are referring to alcoholics and drug addicts. However, it is also true of sex addictions such as unfaithfulness, homosexuality, and internet pornography. In fact, internet pornography is now the number one addiction in the Western World.

II Thessalonians 2:10-12, *"Because they did not receive the love of the TRUTH, that they might be saved, for this reason God will send them strong delusion, that they should believe the lie, that they all may be condemned who did not believe the TRUTH but had pleasure in unrighteousness."*

John 14:6 *Jesus said, "I am the way, the TRUTH, and the life."*

John 8:32 *"The TRUTH will set you free."*

I John 1:8 *"If we say we have no sin, we deceive ourselves and the TRUTH is not in us."*

I beg you to receive the TRUTH because I want you to be spared the consequences of refusing to believe the TRUTH.

CHAPTER 32
PROGRESSIVE CHANGE VERSUS MORAL ABSOLUTES

Perhaps you are wondering why I am spending so much time writing about the negative, lowdown, dirty, cheap, ugly, destructive, immoral, debase, perverted, depraved aspects of what the Creator intended to be beautiful, wonderful, thrilling, fulfilling, and exciting.

The truth of the matter is I really do not enjoy writing about the negative. However, it is my intent to clearly convey the truth about the mess human beings have made of God's beautiful design for a wonderful, intimate sexual relationship between a man and a woman in marriage.

Man in his humanness has rejected God who created us in His own image. Instead man has been working overtime via cut and paste to reverse God's plan by creating God in man's image. Some humanistic religions have gone to the extreme trying to convince us we can believe whatever we want about God that God will accept their humanistic beliefs. Also, man thinks he can practice our sexuality however we please. Take it from me, a counselor, we have made a mammoth mess of God's beautiful plan.

Proverbs 14:12 "There is a way that seems right to a man, but the end thereof are the ways of death." Those of liberal persuasion may call themselves Progressives and they may call their liberal attitudes toward sex and modern families' progression, but that does not change God's standards of moral absolutes. Progressives are doing everything in their power including seeking help from Legislators, Congress, the court system, ACLU, and the President of the United States to turn the tables on the proclaimers of God's truth. They promote deviant unnatural sexual behavior as progress. They accuse Conservatives of being against progress and against diversity. They say we use hate language when speaking about people who have a different sexual orientation other than the beautiful plan God, the Creator, gave us. They call the truths that we quote from God's Word hate speech.

The following is a quote from Ravi Zacharias, "The greatest crisis facing the world today is the unwillingness to face up to the ramifications of the truth." I am convinced that sexual immorality is the number one destructive downfall of the culture. If we are honest, we will have to admit the cost of sexual sin is a huge drain on society and the economy. The following are just a few of the ways we are being impacted monetarily: Medical assistance, law enforcement, prisons, attorneys and courts, as well as costs to families and friends.

CHAPTER 33
PRO-CREATION

As I stated in the letter to the Sentinel, there are two major purposes for sexual intimacy, Pro Creation and Rec Creation. Procreation is God's plan for inhabiting the earth. God told the man to leave his parents and the home where he was raised. God told him to cleave to his wife and the two shall become one emotionally and physically. He told the married couple to bear children and multiply. In fact, he put within young women the mental, emotional, and physical desire to bear children. Yes, I know there are a few who claim they never wanted children and never had the desire to have children. It is not for me to judge their reasons, thoughts, statements, or actions.

There are numerous lesbians and some homosexual men who want children by adoption or other scientific assistance. This is not God's plan. God's plan of one man and one woman in the marriage relationship is perfectly logical, natural, and normal. It is also the plan that God will bless. However, don't get me wrong. There are situations when God blesses adoptions such as traditional families adopting homeless children or families who for various reasons are not able to have children. There is no place in God's Word where He encourages adoptions for people living in a deviant relationship.

In fact, He condemns those relationships. There are those who claim that the U.S. Constitution guarantees equal rights in matters of sexual orientation and adoption. This false, twisted and abusive interpretation of the Constitution is not what our Founding fathers intended. They definitely did not support immorality. When children are born to a husband and wife in a traditional marriage it is a wonderful experience.

The anticipation of the arrival of the new baby or in our case, the births of triplet grandchildren, is one of the most exciting, memorable experiences we have ever had. Although it happened 50 years ago our oldest son, father of the triplets, was born. I remember it as clearly as if it happened yesterday. The doctor walked out of the delivery room (that was before fathers were allowed in the delivery room) and announced, "It's a boy." He followed the announcement by telling me that he had delivered several hundred babies in his practice, yet each time he delivered a new baby, it was like a new miracle.

While we know that babies are the result of a husband and wife coming together in an intimate sexual relationship, apart from God there is no miracle of life.

Throughout the Bible, God uses types, symbols, dreams, visions, and parables to help us better understand the lesson he was trying to convey. When the bride and groom come together in marriage resulting in the birth of a baby, this is a type of something greater. The greater is Christ, (the spiritual groom) and the church (the people of faith) being the bride of Christ, united by the Holy Spirit. As did Paul in First Corinthians, I am taking liberty in sharing the following thoughts.

The sexual union and orgasm between bride and groom may typify the Holy Spirit as the agent between Christ and His Bride. The power of the Holy Spirit working through the bride (the church) that brings about the new spiritual birth of those born into God's family. When one is born into God's family he receives eternal life. This is the birth Jesus spoke of when He told Nicodemus "You must be born again," John 3:3.

Just as we celebrate the birth of our natural children, the angels along with the whole family of God rejoice when one is born again into God's family. When people are considering having their baby aborted, a good question that should be asked is, would Jesus abort one of His babies from the womb prior to being born again into His eternal family? The bride of Christ plays an important role in the birthing of a child into God's family. The bride must also play the role of the spiritual mother (the church) by nursing and nurturing the new babe in Christ.

As a minister and a counselor, I have performed numerous wedding ceremonies and funeral ser-vices. While death and funerals are the result and consequences of sin, including sexual sin, a wedding is a time of optimism, hope, excitement, and celebration. From experience, performing wedding ceremonies is considerably more fulfilling than a funeral service. I never get tired of observing and sharing with the bride and groom in their anticipation and excitement on their wedding day.

Most Christian weddings have a segment in the ceremony that says, "The two shall become one." Bride and groom state their agreement by publicly telling family and friends, that they are committing themselves before God to become ONE physically, emotionally, socially, and spiritually. Thus, begins a lifetime journey of perfecting the ONENESS commitment.

Just as it is God's plan for bride and groom to become one, so it is that the spiritual Bridegroom (Christ) becomes one with us, the Bride (Church). In John's Gospel Chapter 17, Jesus prayed toward the end "that they all may become ONE."

At the wedding, the bride in her beautiful dress takes center-front stage in the presence of family and friends or as stated in the wedding vows before God and these witnesses. The groom is usually the one more nervous yet with great anticipation awaits for the moment to receive his bride as his very own to share their lives together including the marital bed expressed in sexual intimacy. The majority of the people would say the wedding day when practiced according to God's plan is the most exciting day in their life.

In Acts 19:2 the question was asked, "Have you received the Holy Ghost since you believed?" That is akin to asking the question, have you consummated the marriage since you said the wedding vows?

When husband and wife are truly committed to each other until death do them part, the fulfillment of the relationship continues to grow. After the honeymoon, duty calls people to work. When the bride and groom kiss good-bye in the morning, they experience a special sense of well-being that remains with them all day. They feel like they can conquer the world, they can't wait to get home and fall into each other's arms in that special embrace and ultimate intimacy.

CHAPTER 34
REC-CREATION

Just as there are different types of a bride and groom in marriage, there are also a variety of forms of the Holy Spirit such as wind, breath, oil, water, and fire. Terms used for the working of the Holy Spirit in the lives of believers are: Being filled, baptism, and anointing.

When the bride and groom intimately come together as one physically, emotionally, and spiritually for the first time and experience an orgasm, it is very much like a baptism or an overwhelming feeling of oneness. That intensity and euphoric power create a desire for more. It creates a desire to come together again and again. It was God's intention to create a parallel in the experience. To create a parallel to understand the level of intimacy God wants with us spiritually. Just as it is difficult to describe an orgasm, it is hard to explain the encounter with the presence and power of the Holy Spirit. In both cases, it must be experienced, it changes you, and gives an overwhelming sense of God's presence. The power as it pertains to the Holy Spirit signifies an explosion.

An orgasm can be described as an explosion of ecstasy. Sadly, some wives never experience an orgasm; usually it is due to a lack of education by husband or wife or both. Sometimes it is a fear of the unknown, or a fear to let go of control. Similarly, some members of the Bride of Christ never experience the filling of the Holy Spirit. It has been said regarding the Holy Spirit, let go and let God!

In First Corinthians 14 when it talks about the working of the Holy Spirit, it indicates that the individual who is experiencing the work of the Holy Spirit is edified. In addition, those that are ministered to are edified. Edify means to benefit morally or spiritually. If we allow the Holy Spirit, to work through us we are edified, the church benefits, and so does society. When husband and wife honor God in their intimacy, God blesses them. They in turn have a positive impact on all others with whom they have contact. Recently, I read an article that said, "The best thing that parents can do for their children is maintain a fulfilled sex-life." (That does not mean they invite the children into the bedroom.) It means they will be better parents and citizens. The more we understand the significance of sexual intimacy in the natural, the more we will understand the intimacy and connection in a spiritual relationship with God.

Consequently, our oneness with Christ will bring an overwhelming anointing presence and power of the Holy Spirit. If we pull away from the Bridegroom, the joy of the Holy Spirit will be withdrawn. If you do not fully understand the last couple of pages where I made reference to types, symbols, and parables be assured that if you put into practice the principles you do understand you will find a new measure of fulfillment. However, when you do understand the symbolism of human marriage to what man's relationship with Christ can become, it will change your life!

Just as sex was intended to be an expression of love, so also it is a form of God, the Bridegroom, expressing His love through the operation of the Holy Spirit in His bride for both procreation and rec-creation.

CHAPTER 35

FLEE TEMPTATION

We all learn certain lessons in life through experience and consequences. Sometimes the consequences from making decisions that willfully violate God's principles and our own conscience are hard lessons to learn.

Let's take a brief look at a couple of experiences in the lives of two prominent Bible characters, II Samuel chapter 11. David, who is referred to as—"a man after God's own heart" allowed hormones and temptation to overpower his decision-making. He committed adultery with Bathsheba then had her husband, Uriah, murdered so he would not find out about his wife's pregnancy. Both David and Bathsheba lived with severe consequences the rest of their lives. David's sin drove a wedge between himself and God. It also caused ongoing problems within the family and ultimately the death of his son.

Let's contrast Joseph's temptation with that of David's Joseph was approached by Potiphar's wife on more than one occasion persistently seeking sex. Obviously, Potiphar's wife was not happy in her marriage. Joseph was a handsome young man to whom Potiphar's wife was attracted.

A good question for you men: What would you do if a beautiful, powerful young woman threw herself at you? For the women who read this—you, like Potiphar's wife, are in a situation where you can cause a man to commit adultery. What would you do?

Joseph's response is the one we should all pattern our temptation after. Genesis 39:9 "How can I do this GREAT wickedness and sin against God?" God honored Joseph and elevated him even while he was serving prison time unfairly. He did what God tells us to do, "Flee temptation." In simple words we can all understand, run as fast and as far as you can from temptation. These two Bible stories, along with some of my clients' stories, are strong evidence that there are destructive consequences for defiant disobedience of God's principles and laws. Joseph's story tells us God blesses those who obey Him. Deuteronomy 11:26, "Behold I set before you a blessing and a curse, a blessing if you obey the commandments of the Lord your God, and a curse if you do not obey the commandments of the Lord your God." I share this information trusting that you will see the downside of sexual sin and in turn, you will embrace God's plan and spare yourself further destructive consequences.

I am reminded of John Lennon's song "Imagine". It challenges us to imagine a better world from a humanistic perspective. I suggest we imagine a world where all men trust and obey God. For the sake of this treatise, imagine a world where everybody practices sex according to God's perfect plan.

IMAGINE A WORLD IF:
There would be no AIDS
There would be no abortions
There would be no unwanted children
There would be considerably fewer divorces
There would be lower taxes
There would be fewer police
There would be only a few prisons
There would be smaller government on every level
There would be less government intrusion
There would be fewer laws
Children would be safer

The New Testament gives us further advice on how better to handle our hormones, more commonly referred to as a strong sexual urge or desire. First Corinthians 7:9 tells us that if we cannot exercise self-control one should marry. It does not say it is OK to have a sexual encounter outside of marriage. One may experience relief and instant gratification, but God says, "The pleasures of sin are for a little season," in other words, short lived!

Outside of God's plan, guilt, shame, and other consequences follow the pleasure. It is important that we focus our minds on things that are pure, clean, and holy. In so doing we will experience God's protection for those who are celibate and for those who obey God in marriage. Regarding the marriage license, the question often asked is, "how can a piece of paper make a difference?" It is not so much the paper as it is about the attitude. Those who refuse to marry legally are rebelling against parents, the state, and God. Romans, Chapter 1 makes it clear that if we refuse to acknowledge God and ignore His wonderful plan that He gave us for our good, He will give us over to vile passions.

Women will choose to lust after and have sex with their own gender. Men also will leave the natural way of having sex with women and have sex with one another. God called this behavior shameful. God gave them over to a debased mind and further called their behavior an abomination. He said, "I have spoken the truth and warned you of judgment to come but you mocked Me. You thought you could escape my judgment." However, Galatians 6:7 says, "God is not mocked, whatsoever a man soweth, that shall he also reap. Those who sin against Me are worthy of death." As you can see it is not a pretty picture, there is seemingly little hope. America and numerous other countries are experiencing moral decay like nothing we have known since Sodom and Gomorrah.

Last night I was listening to the radio. There was a discussion about the various sites available online where people can go to meet others for dates, friendship, travel, etc. There was even a site where aculterers go to meet other adulterers who mutually are looking for like-minded cheaters. One sexual experience on a fun date can destroy communication and cause a lifetime of heartbreak with guilt, fear, anxiety, depression, and distrust. As a counselor, I can assure you that these people lead a very empty life. They are constantly looking for that experience that will fill the vacuum in their lives.

I am sure you have noticed on several occasions, while making reference to God's plan for our sexuality, I have called it a Beautiful plan. When practiced according to God's plan it is beautiful. When man selfishly violates God's plan it turns ugly. I interviewed a man who previously had been active in the gay community, regularly visiting gay bars. After sharing with me his experience, using the word "gay" he said was deceitful, but the word "ugly" is not strong enough. Is it any wonder God called sexual sin evil, vile, debased, debauchery, and an abomination.

Adultery (pornea) is the only commandment that when broken encapsulates the other nine commandments.

CHAPTER 36

HOMOSEXUALITY

Homosexuality, being a major political issue, demands more attention than the other sex related issues. Eventually, I think you will understand why.

Tom Robinson said, "Make no mistake, sin is sin, and God's word condemns all forms of sexual sin, including adultery, fornication, and pornography. However, what is especially shocking in modern societies' war against God is how homosexual activity has gone from behavior practiced behind closed doors to being advocated by government and flaunted in main street parades. Does anyone care how God views this?"

Questions of why, when, where, and how regarding homosexuality have been asked and continue to be asked since God created mankind. These same questions played a prominent role in my writing a paper on the homosexual matrix 39 years ago while working on my doctoral degree in Human Behavior.

In my pursuit of trying to find answers, I visited several libraries on university campuses in Southern California. I read several books on the subject only to become more frustrated in my search for answers. The books I read were written by doctors, psychologists, and psychiatrists. Most of the content in these writings is about patients or clients of these professionals in the mental health branch of medicine. While they did not all agree, most felt homosexuality was a mental illness. This information created a real dilemma for me because it put the Creator and the medical profession at odds. It put God into the position of judging man and punishing him for an illness man did not choose.

In my frustration and quest for answers, a bizarre thought came to me. Why not talk to people who supposedly have this mental illness. I decided to spend time in the gay communities of Los Angeles and Hollywood interviewing numerous gays and lesbians. To put them at ease, I told them I was doing research for a paper I was writing. I told them I did not want their names, phone numbers, or addresses. I just wanted them to be open and honest about their sexual identity.

My strategy seemed to work as my subjects were relaxed and honest. I interviewed numerous gays and lesbians and a few bisexuals and transgender. I obtained valuable information that I was not able to get from the books I had read. I learned there were several different circumstances that lead people to get involved in a homosexual lifestyle. In the case of most of those I interviewed, they admitted there was emptiness in their lives, and they were searching for answers. There were different times and ways they were introduced to someone who was already a practicing homosexual. In their search to fill the vacuum in their lives, out of curiosity, they began to experiment. A few of them told me their first homosexual experience was a result of being forced. Quite a few of them admitted to being very angry for various reasons. Their getting involved in the gay community was the result of rebellion, sometimes toward parents, sometimes toward society, and a few said they were angry with God. They exhibited an attitude of "nobody is going to tell me how to live my life."

I talked to a couple of young men who told me they had come to Hollywood from the Midwest hoping to make it in show business. While they were quite talented, they found there were hundreds of people trying to make it in the entertainment world. They had no money. They needed jobs and a place to stay. They were given a card and told to go see another agent. The agent turned out to be a pimp. He told them he would provide them with food and a place to stay. He said in the near future he could probably get them an acting job, but in the meantime, they would have to be willing to sell their bodies. Out of desperation, they went along with the scheme and eventually were caught up in the homosexual lifestyle. There were numerous males and females who had had a negative relationship with a parent (more often than not it was the father). This led to a distorted view of the opposite sex. Eventually, somebody of the same sex came into their lives and made them feel important with flattering words of affirmation. In a high percentage of these cases, they knew their parents and peers would not approve of their new lifestyle. This resulted in the homosexual community becoming their support group.

Another factor in large numbers of people looking for fulfillment was the filling of their minds with perverted pornography. Curiosity from what they read along with the visuals led to experimentation. Experimentation and practice leads to addiction. The progression of abnormal, unnatural sexual experimentation is quite similar to experimentation with tobacco, alcohol, and drugs. While a person's first experience, along with their ongoing practices can be quite different, continuing in deviant behaviors leads to addictions.

In my research, I concluded that most peoples' early experiences are not fulfilling. However, just as first experiences with tobacco and alcohol are not enjoyable, eventually the addiction takes control. One hundred percent of the people who suffer from addictions experience guilt, which in turn leads to depression and anxiety. A very high percentage of those who suffer addiction related depression also suffer with suicidal thoughts and sometimes attempts.

It was the mid 70's. Shortly after I completed my research, the American Psychiatric Association concluded homosexuality is a genetic issue with which some people are born. This theory creates an even bigger dilemma for me. It would indicate that God created a small percentage of the population with a gene that causes those with the gene to behave abnormally. In turn, He punishes those people for having the gene that causes their sinful behavior.

Prior to 1978, the American Psychiatric Association said homosexuality was a mental illness. Now they are trying to convince us that it is a normal genetic problem. Not all medical doctors and mental health professionals agree on this issue.

The promoters of this theory have been somewhat successful. They have relentlessly pushed their philosophy through the courts, Legislatures, Congress, and city councils. Just a few months ago, this divisive issue of same sex unions was ramrodded through the city council of my hometown against the will of the majority of its citizens.

An ordinance was passed that gives special rights to people in same sex unions. This arrogant action has divided and polarized our community. This moral issue has now become the number one political focus in our community. The proponents of the social revolution including President Obama have lost their moral compass. Homosexuality is the only sin where those who practice it receive congratulation kudos for their behavior from the President of the United States. If we don't embrace this sin that God called an abomination, we can expect to be ostracized. If we publicly speak out against the sin of homosexuality, we will be vilified and forced to apologize. Homosexuals are noted for saying, "it's not fair that they don't get the same acceptance as heterosexuals." Some have even gone so far as to say, "God is not fair." In trying to gain acceptance, they twist the interpretation of the Bible. They say if God were fair, He would let gays, lesbians, and straight people choose their sexual orientation. Human nature is such that we all want to be in complete control of our life decisions. Truth of the matter is God has given us the power to choose. The problem is homosexuals make the wrong choice when they choose same sex unions.

Homosexuals try hard to convince themselves that if they violate God's plan but get enough people to accept their immoral addictive behavior, everything will be OK. A measure of acceptance may alleviate some shame, but it can never remove the consequences and guilt of one's behavior. They think that full acceptance of their lifestyle will make them feel valued. It seems like yesterday that gays asked to be left alone to practice their sinful behavior in the privacy of their own bedroom.

Homosexuals no longer want to be left alone. They want heterosexuals to accept, approve, endorse, affirm, validate, embrace, and support their deviant, abnormal, unnatural behavior. They want our children to be taught at a very early age that their perverted abnormal behavior is normal. They are doing everything in their power to influence city council members, legislators, congressmen, and judges to help them gain acceptance.

They arrogantly mock the Creator's beautiful plan and ridicule those who embrace traditional marriage of one man and one woman.

I choose to reject that theory. In my understanding of God, all sin involves an act of the will. In other words, man has the power to choose to do right or wrong according to the principles that give us direction and a conscience that God has given us to know right from wrong.

Of course, if we choose to reject God, the all-wise Creator, then I guess we could conclude that homosexuality and other deviant, abnormal, unnatural sexual orientations are a freak of nature. On the other hand, we can embrace the theory of evolution and agree that man is evolving from two genders, male and female, to several new genders. When you stop to think about it, it sounds ridiculous.

The scary part is either man has a major misunderstanding of God, or he just plain chooses to reject God. Either way, he is choosing to believe that which the promoters of same-sex unions teach is normal and deserves the blessing of all religions and support of all Americans

This information is a brief overview from my recollection of the research on my essay of 40 years ago.

Promoters of homosexuality have done an outstanding job of convincing people (especially young people who are confused about their sexuality) about gender orientation, due to false information and indoctrination. They say abnormal, unnatural sexual behavior is who they are. They have purposefully raised the wrong question. The question should not be (Who) it should be (What) and (Why). What are you doing regarding immoral behavior and why have you chosen to reject and mock the Creator's beautiful plan of sexual intimacy in marriage?

Homosexuals try to make us feel that deviant practices are OK as long as safe sex methods are used. However, God has made it very clear there will be justice for such violations of His laws and His principles. In addition to God's judgments, there are numerous consequences for homosexual sins. The following are a few of the consequences:

<u>Emotional consequences</u>: Fear of what members of one's family and friends might think when they find out their loved one is living a perverse lifestyle; fear of contracting a sexually transmitted disease; fear of God's judgment; anxiety, depression, anger, and guilt.

<u>Social consequences</u> Trying to find one's niche in society can be difficult; trying to find acceptance other than in the homosexual community; finding a support system that is uplifting rather than degrading.

Physical consequences: There are numerous sexually transmitted diseases passed around in the homosexual community; while some of them are treatable, many are not curable; the HIV/AIDS virus is considerably more prevalent among homosexuals. Homosexual males are among the leading carriers and transfers of the AIDS virus. I have been told by a few homosexual men who previously frequented gay bars and clubs that a high number of homosexual men have had sex with 500 or more partners, in some cases more than 1000. Some experts on disease control said AIDS is the number one problem in the world today. When I first started counseling, AIDS was not a known disease. However, there were other health related issues due to homosexual behavior. Thirty years ago, the average lifespan for a male homosexual was 39 years. The average age for females was 43 years.

Due to scientific research, there are a number of new medications that have helped prolong the lives of those who practice dangerous sexual behavior. So far, there is no proven cure for AIDS. Approximately 46 million people have died from the AIDS epidemic. One proven way to minimize the AIDS epidemic would be when people with sexually transmitted diseases stop having sexual relations. Also, when people start following God's plan and practice monogamy within the marriage institution of one man and one woman. For these people AIDS will almost be eliminated. Why doesn't the medical profession put more emphasis on monogamy?

I have attended a number of seminars on how to relate to and treat persons who have HIV/AIDS virus. At these seminars, there was considerable discussion on safe sex (use of condoms). While these methods help slow the spread of AIDS we are a long way from being successful in stopping the spread of the disease. However, the success rate with monogamous married couples is almost 100 percent and it is not necessary to use condoms. What is referred to as safe sex is not safe sex at all. It is an attempt at safe sin.

Twenty years ago, we were visiting in a home of some friends. Their son who had contracted AIDS from a celebrity was on his deathbed. The aura of death was overwhelming. It was not a pleasant experience.

Some other friends were traveling in an unfamiliar area in another state away from home. Being a hot summer day, they stopped at a bar to get a cold drink. They entered the facility only to find out they were in a gay bar. They said it was dark and depressing and they could not wait to get out. A client of mine who used to frequent gay bars called them "the dark side".

Financial Consequences – The cost of treating sexually transmitted diseases is astronomical. Most people who acquire HIV end up being bankrupted because of the high cost of medical treatment. In addition, a high percentage of AIDS cases take a toll on the families. The costs are carried over to the local community and to society in general through fundraisers, higher taxes, high insurance premiums, and the public monies channeled through public health districts. We, the people, have no choice. Through higher taxes we are forced to shoulder the costs for sex related sinful behaviors such as AIDS and other sexually transmitted diseases for those in the military and penal system. We should never minimize all of the aforementioned problems and costs related to homosexuality. However, the primary and larger problem is spiritual.

Spiritual Consequences – When man rejects the Creator's perfect plan and violates God's rules that govern sexuality, he will suffer guilt, anxiety, and depression. Leviticus 18 and Romans Chapter 1 tells us what God has to say about homosexual relations. He calls homosexuality an abomination. God says to those who embrace and practice homosexuality, go ahead, do it your way. Go ahead promote your perverted lifestyle by provocatively and blatantly marching down the main streets of our cities. Toronto, my home for 11 years, is now the home for World Pride, the largest annual parade and celebration of homosexuality in the world. A few years ago, we were in Toronto during World Pride Week. I was watching the news. It was all about the gay pride and sexual perversion, the kinds of immoral display that would have never been allowed in public just a few years ago. If you violate God's principles, be prepared to accept the consequences of sin because you are exchanging the truth of God for a lie. The promoters of same sex unions as being normal have done a masterful job in selling the lie.

The violation of God's rules and principles can only be dealt with on the spiritual level. Need I remind you that God's plan is still and will always be the BEST. For those who choose to reject God, logic should tell us that God's plan works a whole lot better.

One can only experience forgiveness through humble confession and repentance; in other words, a complete surrender of our will to God. It has been said that the leading indicator of a nation gone awry is man rejecting the Creator's plan for human sexuality. In so doing, man and his Country set a course of self-destruction.

Let me encourage you to reject the lie and embrace the TRUTH. John 14:6 Jesus said, "I am the TRUTH." John 8:32 "The TRUTH will set you FREE."

Earlier I made reference to homosexual hijacking the word 'gay' from its intended meaning in the English language. They contemptuously have also stolen God's purpose for the beautiful colors in the rainbow. The following is a recent headline in our local newspaper, "A VERY COLORFUL DISPLAY". The article stated that rainbow flags were placed above a new exhibit in the Human Rights Education Institute just in time to celebrate lesbian, gay, bisexual, and transgender pride month.

Today's news—Burger King has caved in to the demands of persistent homosexuals. Burger King will be selling burgers in rainbow wrapping paper.

Homosexuals are out front with rallies and gay rights parades. Another headline in our local newspaper was "Anti-discrimination Legislation Sought". Subtitle says, "Gay Rights Activists Arrested in Idaho Senate." Dozens of activists blocked the entrance to the Idaho Senate chambers. The picture showed the activists blocking the Senate Pro Tem. Idaho State Police took 43 people into custody. The activists are threatening to continue to block the entrance until they get, 'sexual orientation and gender identity' added to the Human Rights Ordinance. Homosexuals are no longer asking for equal rights. They are defiant in their attitudes and behavior toward God, the State, and heterosexuals who choose not to embrace their deviant lifestyle. They want special rights. Recently Hollywood held its Annual Awards Gala. During the awards presentation ceremony, a wedding ceremony was performed for 38 homosexual couples. The whole atmosphere was an attitude of "in your face world." Hollywood recently released a new movie called,

"Corpus Christi" (Body of Christ). The purpose of this movie is to mock Jesus Christ. Homosexuals have rejected the Creator's beautiful plan for marriage and sexual intimacy between a man and a woman.

Disney World is planning for Gay Recognition Day at the Magic Kingdom. They are purposefully and deliberately exposing our children to a deviant lifestyle that just a few years ago was considered sinful and perverted. What was considered sin is now being taught in our public schools as being normal and to be celebrated. The radical homosexuals have a plan to indoctrinate an entire generation of American children with pro-homosexual propaganda and thereby eliminating traditional values from American society altogether. Their plan is to create a new America based on sexual promiscuity via the deceptively named "Student Non-discrimination Act."

Liberals in their accusations of the Right say Conservatives are prudes who are out of touch with reality. Some think Conservatives believe sex is only for procreation. Truth is, God's plan is the reverse of His critics' claims. His plan is for our good! He intended for sex to be pleasurable. Yet anti-God, anti-Christian critics are the ones who denigrate sex. They pervert the plan of the Creator of sex and wonder why they are driven to find fulfillment in deviant sexual practices. They try to improve on God's plan of marriage being a sacred union between one man and one woman.

A few years ago, when Congress was debating the Marriage Amendment, Hillary Clinton said, "Marriage was a sacred union between one man and one woman. Now as a candidate for President of the United States, she has publically endorsed same-sex marriage. After calling marriage a sacred union and now embracing an immoral union that God calls an abomination, it is like a slap in the face. It is mockery of the Creator who designed God's beautiful plan for marriage and sexuality.

A few years ago, I was interviewing a man who had recently left the homosexual community. He told me that prior to leaving that lifestyle his life was a nightmare. He was constantly thinking about and planning for the next sexual encounter. He said his life was one of loneliness, sadness, and pain. The loneliness and sadness was the result of guilt, depression, and broken relationships. The average committed homosexual relationship lasts approximately 2 years.

When questioning him as to how he got into the homosexual lifestyle, he said sexual abuse in childhood played a major role. He said that as many as 75 percent of homosexual males had been sexually abused as a child by another man close to them. A broken relationship with one's father can also play a role in a boy or young man turning to another male. The percentage of lesbians having been abused by a man is even higher, followed by female sexual abuse. While this information is helpful in understanding and working with those seeking help, there is no viable proof that males or females are born with a different orientation. Commonsense and knowledge should tell us that we have made a huge mess of things by trying to improve on God's plan. Some multi-sexual relationships are so entangled it takes a genius of an investigator to get to the bottom of these complex affairs. It sounds like the entanglements of stories on Dateline and 48 hours.

If those who are trying to improve on God's plan are doing so well, why have such a high percentage of homosexuals contemplated suicide? Approximately 41 percent have attempted or seriously considered suicide, mostly because of guilt.

The following personal story should give you further insight as to the confusion that comes from sexual abuse. Hopefully, the person who is telling this story will give those who have had similar experiences a great measure of hope.

Ben's Story

When I was approximately 10 years old, a neighbor boy whom I played with told me he had something he wanted to show me. I followed him to a place where he had hidden a couple of pornographic magazines in a culvert. There were numerous pictures of nudity. At 10 years of age, my curiosity caused me to want to see more. At that early age my conscience made me feel guilty. I felt like I was doing something wrong. My friend told me he found the magazines in his garage. When he went to return the magazines, he found some new ones. He replaced the two magazines and removed two more from the pile. We got together quite often to look at the latest porno magazines, some of these later editions involved same-sex union relationships. The more we viewed the nude pictures, the more we wanted to see the next edition. We were viewing what I now know to be hard core pornography.

During the next five years we started sharing our findings with some other kids. By the time we were fifteen we talked a couple of girls into experimenting. Shortly after these experiences, my parents sent me to a church summer camp. One of the speakers talked about the importance of keeping ourselves pure. The guilt I experienced caused me to ask God to forgive me. It felt like a heavy weight had been lifted from me. I promised God I would never go back to pornography. However, a short time after I returned home I got with my old friends. The temptation was too great, I started viewing porno again. There were more girls. Then one day one of the boys brought to the group some homosexual pornography. There was some experimenting. The guilt feelings were stronger than ever.

I went to summer camp again when I was 17 or 18. I asked for forgiveness again. One speaker challenged us to give our lives to God for service. I wanted to be free from guilt and I wanted to please God. So I told God I wanted to serve Him.

During the next few years I tried hard to please God by living a morally pure life. I was reasonably successful, but periodically I gave into temptation. Ridding those sexual images from my mind seemed impossible.

After high school I went to Bible College to study for the ministry. I thought that being around Christian students and faculty would help get my mind off immoral thoughts and images. It did help, but there were times when I was struggling with my studies I reverted back to my old ways. The guilt overwhelmed me. I considered dropping out of school. I did not give in because I didn't want to admit to my family and friends that I was a failure. Over the years I have heard numerous times that pornography is harmless entertainment. I tried so hard to believe that, only to be overwhelmed with guilt.

During my second year in Bible College I met a nice Christian lady. It was obvious by the twinkle in Ellen's eyes when she looked at me that her interest went beyond a typical friendship. Because of my guilt and fear of Ellen finding out about my addictions, I found myself emotionally withdrawing from the relationship. I missed the warmth of her personality. I tried to allow her to get closer to me. However, because of the guilt factor in my life, our relationship turned into a rollercoaster ride. Yet there was something about our relationship I could not totally break up with Ellen. Eventually we began to share more and more with each other, but the factors regarding my addiction must remain locked in my memory safe forever.

Shortly after graduating from Bible College, we got married. The night of our wedding day things did not go well. The first few days of our marriage were a disaster.

I found myself withdrawing from Ellen. I began to struggle with my feelings as to whether I should share my secret problems with Ellen.

During the first year after graduating from Bible College and getting married to Ellen, I received an invitation to accept a position of Assistant Pastor of a church. Once again, I tried to convince myself that doing spiritual work might very well free me from the thoughts that kept haunting me. Unfortunately I had adverse experiences from what I had hoped for. I was lusting after some members of the church.

During Ellen's first pregnancy I withdrew even more. Ellen felt something was wrong. She began to question me. Being put on the spot, I lied to her. Over the next few years I became a habitual liar. I hated myself. My unhappiness with myself and my marriage drove me back to pornography and several affairs, including a same-sex union affair. The more recent porno caused me to believe I was bisexual. I suffered from deep depression accompanied by suicidal thoughts. Also I got us into debt through credit card spending. I took out two new cards in my name only.

Ellen began checking our mail, email, and phone calls more closely. She discovered information pertaining to my secret life. Upon further questioning, I broke down, cried, and told her everything regarding my past. I begged Ellen not to leave me. I needed her. I am presently getting help from a counselor. In counseling I have learned that my addictions are learned behavior. Unfortunately the deviant behavior I learned as a child and teenager practically destroyed my life, and the lives of my wife and children. I learned that I have to answer to God, the Creator of my sexuality. I have asked God, my wife, and the members of my church to forgive me. Although I am still dealing with some guilt and unwanted thoughts, for the first time in years I am feeling an amazing sense of freedom.

Ben

Recently Ben told me he feels he is conquering the demon. I assured him with God's help and a good support system he could win this battle and be free from his past.

(Did you notice that Ben referred to his deviant sexual practices as addictions?) Along with Ben, it is my desire that those of you who have read this story of his journey will be encouraged. For those of you whose lives are broken and you are still struggling with the addiction to homosexuality, we pray that your lives will be transformed resulting in being set free from bondage and the accompanying grip of guilt and shame.

The next story gives us another perspective of some of the devastating problems caused by people who decide to change their orientation.

I have known Shirley's family for 38 years. I have witnessed some of the deep emotional pain that members of the family continue to endure. While I have not been close to the children, my communication was with their mother and grandmother. The children are the ones who are terribly confused and hurt the most.

Shirley's Story

Every time a new state redefines marriage, the news is full of happy stories of gay and lesbian couples and their new families.

But behind those big smiles and sunny photographs are other, more painful stories. These are left to secret, dark places. They are suppressed, and those who would tell, are silenced in the name of "marriage equality."

I represent one of those real life stories that are kept in the shadows. I have personally felt the pain and devastation wrought by the propaganda that destroys natural families.

The Divorce

In the fall of 2007, my husband of almost ten years told me that he was gay and wanted a divorce. In an instant, the world that I had known and loved—the life we had built together—was shattered.

I tried to convince him to stay, to stick it out and fight for our marriage. But my voice, my desires, my needs—and those of our two young children—no longer mattered to him. We had become disposable, because he had embraced one tiny word that had become his entire identity. Being gay trumped commitment, vows, responsibility, faith, fatherhood, marriage, friendships, and community. All of this was thrown away for the sake of his new identity.

Try as I might to save our marriage, there was no stopping my husband. Our divorce was not settled in mediation or with lawyers. No, it went all the way to trial. My husband wanted primary custody of our children. His entire case can be summed up in one sentence: "I am gay, and I deserve my rights." It worked: the judge gave him practically everything he wanted. At one point, he even told my husband, "If you had asked for more, I would have given it to you."

I truly believe that judge was legislating from the bench, disregarding the facts of our particular case and simply using us— using our *children*—to help influence future cases. In our society, LGBT citizens are seen as marginalized victims who must be protected at all costs, even if it means stripping rights from others. By ignoring the injustice committed against me and my children, the judge seemed to think that he was correcting a larger injustice.

My husband had left us for his gay lover. They make more money than I do. There are two of them, and only one of me. Even so, the judge believed that they were the victims. No matter what I said or did, I didn't have a chance of saving our children from being bounced around like so many pieces of luggage.

A New Same-Sex Family—Built On The Ruins of Mine

My ex-husband and his partner went on to marry. Their first ceremony took place before our state redefined marriage. After it created same-sex marriage, they chose to have a repeat performance. In both cases, my children were forced—against my will and theirs—to participate. At the second ceremony, which included more than twenty couples, local news stations and papers were on hand to document the first gay weddings officiated in our state. *USA Today* did a photo journal shoot of my ex and his partner, my children, and even their grandparents. I was not notified that this was taking place, nor was I given a voice to object to our children being used as props to promote same-sex marriage in the media.

At the time of the first ceremony, the marriage was not recognized by our state, our nation, or our church. And my ex-husband's new marriage, like a majority of male-male relationships, is an "open," non-exclusive relationship. This sends a clear message to our children: what you feel trumps all laws, promises, and higher authorities. You can do whatever you want, whenever you want—and it doesn't matter who you hurt along the way.

After our children's pictures were publicized, a flood of comments and posts appeared. Commentators exclaimed at how beautiful this gay family was and congratulated my ex-husband and his new partner on the family that they "created." But there is a significant person missing from those pictures: the mother and abandoned wife. That "gay family" could not exist without me.

There is not one gay family that exists in this world that was created naturally. Every same-sex family can only exist by manipulating nature. Behind the happy façade of many families headed by same-sex couples, we see relationships that are built from brokenness. They represent covenants broken, love abandoned, and responsibilities crushed. They are built on betrayal, lies, and deep wounds.

This is also true of same-sex couples who use assisted reproductive technologies such as surrogacy or sperm donation to have children. Such processes exploit men and woman for their reproductive potential, treat children as produce to be bought and sold, and purposely deny children a relationship with one or both of their biological parents. Wholeness and balance cannot be found in such families, because something is always missing. *I am* always missing, But *I am real*, and I represent hundreds upon thousands of spouses who have been betrayed and rejected.

If my husband had chosen to stay, I know that things wouldn't have been easy. But that is what marriage is about: making a vow and choosing to live it out, day after day. In sickness and in health, in good times and in bad, spouses must choose to put the other person first, loving them even when it's hard.

A good marriage doesn't only depend on sexual desire, which can come and go and is often out of our control. It depends on choosing to love, honor, and be faithful to one person, forsaking all others. It is common for spouses to be attracted to other people— usually of the opposite sex, but sometimes of the same sex. Spouses who value their marriage do not act on those impulses. For those who find themselves attracted to people of the same sex, staying faithful to their opposite-sex spouse isn't a betrayal of their true identity. Rather, it's a decision not to let themselves be ruled by their passions. It shows depth and strength of character when such people remain true to their vows, consciously striving to remember, honor, and revive the love they had for their spouses when they first married.

My Children Deserve Better

Our two young children were willfully and intentionally thrust into a world of strife and combative beliefs, lifestyles, and values, all in the name of "gay rights." Their father moved into his new partner's condo, which is a complex inhabited by sixteen gay men.

One of the men has a 19-year-old male prostitute who comes to service him. Another man, who functions as the father figure of this community, is in his late sixties and has a boyfriend in his late twenties. My children are brought to gay parties where they are the only children and where only alcoholic beverages are served. They are taken to transgender baseball games, gay rights fundraisers, and LGBT film festivals.

Both of my children face identity issues, just like other children. Yet there are certain deep and unique problems that they will face as a direct result of my former husband's actions. My son is now a maturing teen, and he is very interested in girls. But how will he learn how to deal with that interest when he is surrounded by men who seek sexual gratification from other men? How will he learn to treat girls with care and respect when his father has rejected them and devalues them? How will he embrace his developing masculinity without seeing his father live out authentic manhood by treating his wife and family with love, honoring his marriage vows even when it's hard?

My daughter suffers too. She needs a dad who will encourage her to embrace her femininity and beauty, but these qualities are parodied and distorted in her father's world. Her dad wears make-up and sex bondage straps for Halloween. She is often exposed to men dressing as women. The walls in his condo are adorned with large framed pictures of women in provocative positions. What is my little girl to believe about her own femininity and beauty? Her father should be protecting her sexuality. Instead, he is warping it.

Without the guidance of both their mother and their father, how can my children navigate their developing identities and sexuality? I ache to see my children struggle, desperately trying to make sense of their world.

My children and I have suffered great losses because of my former husband's decision to identify as a gay man and throw away his life with us. Time is revealing the depth of those wounds, but I will not allow them to destroy me and my children. I refuse to lose my faith and hope. I believe so much more passionately in the power of marriage covenant between one man and one woman today than when I was married. There is another way for those with same-sex attractions. Destruction is not the only option—it cannot be. Our children deserve far better from us.

Shirley

This type of devastation should never happen to another spouse or child. Please, I plead with you: defend marriage as being between one man and one woman. We must stand for marriage—and for the precious lives that marriage creates.

In the past people who chose to live a deviant perverted lifestyle quietly kept their sexual activities to themselves and their partners. Then came the hijacking of the beautiful descriptive word "GAY" from our vocabulary. Now it is used to label a bizarre perverted lifestyle. About the same time homosexuals started coming out of the closet they also started using their new title. That which was socially unacceptable in America for 200 years (even considered criminal behavior) became socially acceptable behavior. This was followed by socially acceptable diseases; Aids, etc. and socially acceptable death.

Those who died from Aids were deemed courageous and died with a badge of honor. This statement was not intended to diminish the value of their lives. Now they are doing everything in their power to force society to accept their behavior as normal. They say straight people have politicized the issue. NOT SO!!! Supporters of homosexuality have taken a moral issue and politicized it by using the courts, Legislatures, and Congress as part of their strategy to win the political battle. They have left us with no other choice but to defend natural, normal, traditional marriage through the system for the sake of our children and grandchildren.

CHAPTER 37

HOMOPHOBIA

The first paragraph is a description of homophobia by those who believe homosexuality is normal. Homophobia is experienced as feelings of fear, discomfort, dislike, hatred, or disgust with same sex sexuality. Homophobia also destroys families when parents discover one of their children is lesbian, gay, or bisexual. They say it would be much better to preserve family unity by supporting and honoring all relatives regardless of their sexual orientation or affection preference. For far too long, exotic and sexual contact between women and men has been thought of as a major social problem. However, they say the problem is not homosexuality. They say the real issue is homophobia.

Basically what they are saying is the sin of homosexuality is not the destroyer of families. The destroyer is the fear and hatred of same sex unions. This is an obvious admission of exchanging truth for a lie.

President Obama and Attorney General Eric Holder have issued memorandums granting a special status to "transgendered" persons. To you, parents, how will you respond to your young children when they come home from school and ask why a cross-dressing male teacher is wearing girl clothes? Perhaps just as important a question, what kind of answer will you be allowed to give your innocent children that is politically correct, and not considered hate speech?

Are these children homophobic because of their uncomfortable feelings about the strange behavior of their teacher? Did they inherit homophobia from their parents or did they contract this disease from their peers or parents? Perhaps God created them with a conscience, commonsense, and a logical mind so when observing abnormal behavior their innocent minds recognize it as unnatural. Are your teenage daughters homophobic because they feel uncomfortable when a teenage boy enters the girl's restroom wearing a mini skirt claiming he is transgendered?

In the chapter on Sex Slave Trade, I quoted Jesus as He said, "If we offend a child, a millstone should be hung around his neck and he should be thrown into the water and drowned." I believe this also applies to the offenders of children when they are purposely given false information regarding their sexuality. I quote this again because it tells us how much Jesus hates the abuses of innocent children. These are strong words!! They make people who do not want to hear God's truth about their sexuality, angry. In their anger, they twist the truth and place the blame on those who speak the truth by blaming them for the homosexuals' anxiety, depression, guilt, and sometimes suicide.

When someone takes a public stand for truth and right behavior against homosexuality he/she is labeled homophobic. The following are excerpts from a flier I picked up at a Gay, Lesbian, and Bi-sexual Conference. Hopefully this information will help you better understand why homosexuals make accusations and label heterosexuals as having the disease called homophobia. Their definition of homophobia: Is the fear of feelings of love for members of one's own gender; prejudice based on personal belief that lesbian, gay, and bi-sexual people are sinful, immoral, sick, and inferior to heterosexuals.

They claim their behavior is not the problem and their lifestyle is not by choice. I suggest they explain how this so-called disease called homophobia is a choice. Hundreds of millions of people when they see homosexuals embracing and kissing get a queasy feeling when observing this bizarre behavior. This feeling by heterosexuals toward this strange, perverted behavior is not a choice. Why shouldn't homosexuals have to be tolerant of people who are homophobic when they were born with homophobia? We all have a conscience and we all know right from wrong. Homosexuals choose wrong!!

Homophobia is the label homosexuals place on those who do not accept the inclusion of perverted same gender sex when speaking of diversity. While Jesus spoke to the justice side of what perverts deserve for sexually abusing children He also offers hope and redemption for those who humbly come to Jesus like little children. The following is Jesus' own words: "I tell you the truth, unless you become converted and become as little children you will never enter the kingdom of Heaven." Matthew 18:3

CHAPTER 38
NATURAL MARRIAGE

The following are reasons we must win the battle for natural marriage as copied by permission from the Family Research Council publication, March 20, 2014.

Ten Reasons Why Natural Marriage Matters

1. "Marriage is based on the biological fact that reproduction depends on a man and a woman, and the reality that children need a mother and a father."

2. "Marriage is the building block of all human civilization and benefits society in a way that no other relationship does."

3. "Studies consistently show that children do better when raised by a married mom and dad. Redefining marriage will hurt children."

4. "Without both moms and dads, families more often depend on welfare."

5. "Redefining marriage defies Biblical truth. It denigrates marriage to whatever whim the government or the culture say it is."

6. "Pushing out traditional views on the family leads to erosion of religious liberty."

7. "Redefining marriage makes marriage about adult desires instead of the needs of children."

8. "Natural marriage is society's best guarantee of a limited government that stays out of family life."

9. "Extending marriage to same-sex couples will eventually lead to defining virtually every emotional relationship, including polygamy and polyamory as 'marriage'."

10."The redefinition of marriage will arm the government to coerce Christians to recognize and affirm same-sex relationships."

The late D. James Kennedy, Ph.D. said, "Nothing in our popular culture has been more singularly harmful to the healthy development of families in society than the myth that illicit sex can be safe and fulfilling."

It is a proven fact that the best way to improve society is to improve its families. "As the family goes so goes society."

Recent studies support the proposition that natural marriage promotes physical health, mental and emotional health, sexual health, and social productivity. Therefore, it should be the responsibility of society to promote traditional marriage.

Another traditional family supported institution is the Boy Scouts. The Boy Scouts have been infiltrated aggressively by militant homosexuals. They have changed this wholesome organization forever. The same propaganda that penetrated the Boy Scouts is now being perpetrated by the sex education classes in our schools. The dishonest perverted propaganda is causing confusion and is corrupting the minds of our precious children.

Research shows that natural marriage positively impacts the sexual health of individuals. Not only are persons less likely to experience sexual dysfunction, they are more likely to be sexually satisfied with their spouse. Marriage also reduces anxiety, significantly, that only non-monogamous individuals face—the fear of sexually transmitted diseases. Cohabitating unmarried women are more likely to suffer physical and sexual abuse. In addition, sexually transmitted diseases are among the most covered-up illnesses.

Step-fathers are seven times more likely to sexually abuse their step-children than natural fathers in the home.

Children raised in single parent families are more than twice as likely to get in trouble with the law.

The exciting news in Northwest sports is the announcement of Seattle Seahawks' quarterback, Russell Wilson's engagement to his girlfriend. Immediately after the announcement they said they were both Christians and would not be sexually intimate until the wedding day. What a refreshing announcement! Because of their obedience to God they can expect God to bless their marriage.

CHAPTER 39
POLITICS AND IMMORALITY

The intent of this book was never to be political. However, the Progressive liberal left, including the President of the United States and former Governor Andrus have drawn the citizens of Idaho and America into two debates over issues I have written about in previous chapters. These issues are the murdering of approximately 57 million innocent babies and the perversion of sex. These moral issues should not have been politicized. However, since we have been drawn into the fray, it is the responsibility of all of us to seek the truth, stand firm, and fight for what is right. These are not civil or human rights issues. These are moral issues for which all of us will have to answer to God.

The question is, how did so many people so easily get deceived in their thinking that we actually gave mothers the so-called civil right to murder their babies with the assistance and support of Planned Parenthood and some medical doctors? Likewise, how has such a small percentage of the population been able to convince so many to participate in destroying the culture through the promotion of sexual immorality.

President Obama is becoming more and more obsessed with his agenda of forcing the acceptance of homosexuality and other deviant sexual behaviors on the American people. In his speech at the Lyndon B. Johnson Library, he said, "the story of America is about progress" as he made reference to same sex unions. What is happening in America now is not progress. Progress is when things happen for the betterment of society.

Now the President is meddling in the affairs of other countries by promoting his homosexual rights agenda through American embassies. Some diplomats are even taking part in parades and are flying the rainbow flag next to the stars and stripes. The President appointed six openly gay ambassadors last year. Less than twenty years ago, you could be thrown out of Foreign Service for being openly gay. Less than twenty years later, six openly gay ambassadors gathered in Washington D.C. to celebrate progress. They discussed how far the Foreign Service, the nation, and the world has come on the issue of equality, Washington Post, March 25, 2015. They are supporting gay rights in countries such as Poland, Russia, and Nigeria. Can you imagine how God who created male, female, and sexuality feels about the President's appointments?

What a contrast between our present President and Abraham Lincoln (one of our greatest presidents) who acknowledged God in the affairs of man. His personal life and leadership were based on the foundation of God's Word. President Lincoln left us with three basic principles to govern ourselves: (1) Personal responsibility including the area of our sexuality. (2) Lower taxes and (3) Less government. If we discipline ourselves sexually the way God intended, there would be less taxes and less government.

Also, President Obama in his speech at the Lyndon B. Johnson Library quoted Martin Luther King, Jr. by saying, "We shall overcome." The only way we will overcome is by repenting of our sins and by putting God's principles into practice in our lives. In 2 Chronicles 7:14, "If My people who are called by My name will humble themselves and pray and seek My face and turn from their wicked ways, then will I hear from heaven and will forgive their sins and heal their land."

Twenty-five years ago while serving in the Idaho Legislature, the most important issue we were dealing with in the Legislative session was abortion, the killing of innocent babies. A small group of us Conservatives spent days working with Constitutional attorneys trying our best to get the right wording in a solid pro-life bill. The bill was discussed thoroughly in the House and Senate Committees. It was also debated passionately on the floor of the House and Senate. It was voted on and passed both bodies. It was the strongest Pro-life Bill to pass through any State Legislature.

The action we took made national news. Governor Cecil Andrus said he was pro-life. We felt really good about the direction our state was going. All we needed was the Governor's signature and Legislation would become law. Being pro-life we assumed he would sign the bill.

A few weeks later, we finished our work in the House of Representatives. I had already packed my car and was ready to head home to Coeur d'Alene 400 miles north of our State Capitol in Boise. We were waiting for an amended bill to come back from the Senate so we could vote and adjourn the session Sine Die. While waiting, I stepped out to the men's room. I heard a noise outside, so I went to the window and cranked it open a few turns. There were several mobile media units circling the Capitol building. Immediately I knew something important was about to happen. I went back into the House chambers. I asked Tom Boyd, Speaker of the House, if he knew what was happening. He said, "No." I told him I had a funny feeling that the Governor was going to veto our pro-life bill. Approximately 30 minutes later, the amended bill came back from the Senate. We voted and immediately adjourned. I got into my car and started driving north out of Boise. I had not driven more than 12-15 minutes when it came over the radio that the Governor was going to make an announcement. He came on and said he was going to veto the bill. He said that after having it examined by his liberal attorneys it did not pass Constitutional muster. My heart sank into my stomach. I lost respect for Governor Andrus.

Personally, I believe Gov. Andrus philosophically is pro-life. He just did not have the backbone to take a stand for what he knew was morally right. He caved in to the liberal abortion lobbyists. If what he said was true, he could have told us and we could have gotten the attorneys from both sides together to resolve any questionable Constitutional problems. It was obvious this was his plan all along. He could not wait, within 20 minutes after the Legislature adjourned the session Sine Die he vetoed our pro-life bill. He vetoed it after we adjourned so we could not override his veto.

There were correspondents from all over the U.S. and a few other countries present for this historic event.

From time to time during my time in the Legislature, some political maneuvering took place and left me questioning the integrity of some Legislators and lobbyists.

The deceptive action by the Governor was game playing at its best. Deceit destroyed my trust in a number of elected officials who were supposed to be representing the people who elected them to office. Periodically Conservatives and frequently Progressive politicians tend to govern by the philosophy "the end justifies the means." This makes it difficult to know when and whom you can trust. Harry Reid, U.S. Senator from Nevada, is a good example of a politician practicing this philosophy.

It was my privilege to give input to the wording of the Marriage Amendment. Homosexual activists are pressuring city councils and school boards to pass ordinances and change policies that give special rights to gays and lesbians.

Ten years ago, I was invited to testify before the State Affairs Committee of the Idaho Legislature in regard to placing an amendment supporting traditional marriage in the Idaho Constitution. I was asked to be an expert witness on this issue because of an essay I had written on the homosexual matrix back in the mid 70's. A portion of my research was the result of interviewing numerous gays and lesbians in the gay community in Hollywood and Los Angeles.

Due to philosophical differences of the committee, I tried to stay away from dealing with the subject from a religious perspective. I tried to deal with it from a commonsense point of view using words like traditional, practical, natural, and normal. With caution, I tried to be tactful and considerate of the feelings of the people on all sides of this emotionally charged issue. The chairman of the committee at the beginning of the hearing requested that the audience show respect to all who were present by not cheering, applauding, or verbalizing feelings and thoughts. However, some militants showed no respect. Despite further urging by the chairman, they still continued cheering and jeering. One obvious trait of both homosexual men and lesbians is high percentages are very angry. In spite of my careful attempt to handle this subject, gracefully and with dignity, I was still given some unflattering labels such as the "most dangerous person in Idaho."

By the way, we got the Marriage Amendment Bill (after 3 years of trying) out of the State Affairs Committee by one vote. The Amendment then passed through the House and the Senate.

A few days after testifying before the State Affairs Committee, Kate and I flew to Toronto to see our newborn triplet grandchildren. Being there to help bring them home from the hospital was one of the highlights of my life. The thrill of seeing and holding a newborn baby is an experience that one never forgets. When it is your own flesh and blood, it changes your life forever. Holding grandkids is not quite the same as if it were your own. However, holding three new babies was really extra-special.

I am sure you are wondering why I am sharing this story with you. What does it have to do with the subject of the book?

My brother-in-law was the pastor of a church in Ontario, Canada. A couple of days after we brought the triplets home from the hospital he asked me to speak at his church. The Saturday prior to speaking for my brother-in-law, I was sitting at my son's dining room table preparing a sermon. From the time we arrived in Canada, ninety percent of my thoughts were preoccupied with the triplets. Suddenly a thought came to me. Speak on the 'New Birth' from John's Gospel Chapter 3, verses 3 and 4. About that time, I heard something hit the entry door of my son's home. I went to the door and saw the paperboy walking away. There were two newspapers lying on the step. One was a daily and the other was a weekly publication. I took a quick glance and noticed the largest headline I have ever seen on both newspapers. I cannot remember the exact wording. It was something like this: Parliament Passes into Law Same Sex Marriage. Listening to the news the next few days it was obvious that this was a very divisive action.

Back to preparing my sermon, I had very mixed feelings about speaking on the New Birth. The question that came to me was, what kind of life do these new babies have to look forward to when history is made by Parliament in support of immorality? That was eleven years ago. We in America are now following the footsteps of Canada. Legislatures, Congressmen, State and Federal Courts, and even the President of the United States are supporting deviant sexual behavior. This is nothing short of mocking our All Wise God who designed male and female to complement each other through a beautiful plan of sexual intimacy. Do we really think we can improve on the Creator's wonderful plan?

God created Adam and Eve. He made them to enjoy the beauty of each other, in the nude, and they were not ashamed. God placed them in the beautiful Garden of Eden and gave them one rule to obey. He made it clear it was for their own good. However, along came (the conniver he is) in the form of a snake. His tactics were very clear. He questioned Eve in such a way as to make her believe that God was withholding something from her. She shared these words with Adam. Together they decided to find out what they were missing. Immediately they were ashamed. They lost their innocence by testing God. As a marriage counselor, it never ceases to amaze me that when a spouse commits adultery, the offending spouse does not want to be seen in the nude by his/her mate.

That Sunday morning I did preach on the New Birth, making reference to what life would probably be like for these precious newborn triplets in the near future. I read from Romans chapter 1, verses 21-28. After the service that morning an elderly man in his 80's quietly spoke to me. He said he agreed with me in what I had to say regarding homosexuality being an abomination. He followed by saying, "If the right person happened to be in attendance this morning, I could have been arrested for hate speech, for quoting God's word." Just a few weeks later, March 4, 2005, Chris Kempling, a Canadian minister, was arrested and jailed for quoting the Bible. Now in America, ministers are being threatened that they will lose their tax-exempt status for quoting from the Bible or for speaking the truth regarding moral issues such as abortions and same sex unions. Military chaplains have been told they cannot use hate speech, which means they can't quote texts about homosexuality from the Bible. In addition, some chaplains have been told they cannot use Jesus' name when praying.

Today Americans have moved from putting their trust in God to putting their trust in government. However, it hasn't always been that way. The majority of our Founding Fathers believed that the laws of man work only when under the laws of God.

George Washington said, "It is impossible to govern without God and the Bible."

Abraham Lincoln said, "But for (the Bible) we could not know right from wrong. All things most desirable for man's welfare are to be found portrayed in it."

Harry Truman said, "The basis of our Bill of Rights comes from teachings we get from Exodus and St. Matthew, from Isaiah and St. Paul. I don't think we emphasize that enough these days. If we don't have a proper fundamental moral background, we will finally end up with a government which does not believe in rights for anybody except the State."

Progressive political activists are pressuring the majority of people to accept their immorality under the guise of promoting equality, diversity, gender identity, human rights, and sexual orientation. They argue that these terms define who they are rather than what they do. Should not the God who created us be the One who determines who we are? Progressives choose to reject the Truth regarding homosexual behavior. They go so far as to say the U.S. Constitution protects homosexuals from discrimination. They have done a great job selling to society their sexual orientation as being "who they are."

We are told that we cannot censor immorality. However, it really comes down to where we draw the line on censorship. Most of us will agree that pedophilia and bestiality are not acceptable. Some of us agree that all sexual behavior outside God's Plan is a sin.

While I am a strong believer in human rights and diversity, I do not believe that humans should be forced to embrace sinful, perverted and deviant sexual behavior as normal.

Dr. Alan Keyes, Former Ambassador to the U.N. said, "the attack we are now seeing on the people, insisting we embrace so-called homosexual 'marriage', is far more grievous than that which lead the First generation of Americans to declare their independence from Great Britain!"

In the beginning, the first book of the Bible, Genesis, we read about God's creation. At the end of each of the five days of speaking into being His creation, God said, "It was good." On the sixth day, He created Adam and Eve. He said, "It was VERY good." God joined them together as one. He then gave them a list of responsibilities. He told them to take care of the plants and animals in the Garden of Eden. He then gave them one rule. He told them they could eat the fruit of all the trees except one. However, along came Satan in the form of a serpent. He being the cunning, questioning, and lying creature caused Adam and Eve to doubt.

They disobeyed God and immediately realized they were naked. They felt shame, which caused them to make coverings for their nude bodies. They felt guilt and tried to hide themselves from God. It is disturbing to review the direction and how far we have taken it the past 50 years. When I was a teenager, a young lady in a local high school got pregnant out of wedlock. Everything was hush-hush. The family made arrangements for her to leave the community until the baby was born and adopted. A headline story in the news was about a two-page spread in a high school yearbook in Arizona. It was all about celebrating the motherhood of those students who had given birth to babies but were continuing their education. On the plus side, these girls did not abort their babies. The difference between now and 50 years ago is there is no shame in having sex outside of marriage. Now we glamorize sex and motherhood outside of marriage. We make light of immorality and celebrate shameful behavior. Fornication and adultery are celebrated and promoted on TV, in the movies, on the internet, and in novels. A few years ago, the late Michael Landon's TV serial, Little House on the Prairie, was referred to as a model of excellence for family entertainment. Recently his son, Michael Jr., when referring to the lack of restraint in Hollywood regarding the infiltrating of objectionable content in entertainment said, "When you are constantly immersed in this dark, offensive entertainment there is no way it can't affect you."

Lately, every few days articles pertaining to various kinds of deviant sexual behaviors are appearing in newspapers and blogs all over the country. The following are a few recent titles of articles in Idaho newspapers, "Caldwell City Councilman Facing Sex Charge"—the issue had to do with sexual battery of a minor. "Woman Facing Sexual battery Charge"—she had inappropriate sexual contact with a teenage boy. "Groups Urge Court to Intervene in Gay Marriage Dispute"— religions are asking the Supreme Court to intervene. Same sex marriage is a moral issue, not a human rights issue. President Obama during his first campaign for President said marriage should be between a man and a woman. Three years later, he changed his position and now supports same sex marriage. This was verified when Rev. Louie Gigleo was asked to give the benediction at President Obama's second inauguration. Gay rights activists discovered that approximately 20 years earlier Rev. Gigleo preached a sermon calling homosexuality sin, resulting in the inaugural committee and the White House asking him to withdraw from the program. This action made it clear the President embraces sin over the Truth that sets us free. In Romans 1:25-27, "God gave rebellious men over to uncleanness through the lusts of their own hearts, to dishonor their own bodies between themselves. They changed the truth of God into a lie; they worshipped and served the creature more than the Creator. For this cause God gave them up unto vile affections. For even their women did change the natural use into that which is against nature, likewise also the men leaving the natural use of the woman, burned in their lust one toward another; men with men working that which is unseemly (that which is sinful behavior).

History substantiates (verifies) that societies who embrace homosexual behavior cannot survive. Greek and Roman Empires are examples of societal collapse due to moral decline.

"If we or our posterity...live always in the fear of God and shall respect His commandments...we may have the highest hopes of the future fortunes of our country...But if we...neglect religious instruction and authority; violate the rules of eternal justice, trifle with the injunctions of morality, and recklessly destroy the Constitution which holds us together, no man can tell how sudden a catastrophe may overwhelm us and bury all our glory in profound obscurity."
Daniel Webster

Daniel Webster is one of my favorites of the Founding Fathers. I respect him highly for his philosophy, theology, and character.

The story of Sodom and Gomorrah and the decadent perverted lifestyle of their citizens should tell us about God's attitude toward those who mock His creation, His laws, His principles, His character, and

His person. In this account, a group of sex-crazed homosexual perverts demanded that Lot turn over the two angels (God's messengers) for their deviant sexual pleasure. Lot being somewhat afraid of God's judgment, out of desperation, offered his two virgin daughters to the men of Sodom. God told Lot to take his family, get out of this wicked city, and not look back as He was going to destroy Sodom and Gomorrah. Lot's wife disobeyed and God judged her by turning her into a pillar of salt. In the culture at that time, it was extremely important to carry on the family name.

Since Lot did not have any sons and his wife was deceased, his two daughters decided to help God out and carry on Lot's family heritage. Together they conspired to get their father drunk. While in his state of drunkenness, they had sexual intercourse with him according to Genesis 19:11. I cannot help but believe that this was God's consequential judgment on Lot for offering his daughters to these evil men. The sons that were born to his daughters became the tribes of Ammonites and Moabites. The Bible tells us the Ammonites and Moabites practiced child sacrifice and temple prostitution in their ritual worship of idols.

Throughout history, they became enemies to the descendants of Abraham, Isaac, Jacob, and David. This story should be a warning to us as to the importance of being obedient to God with our sexuality.

The proponents of today's liberal philosophy are trying to execute change by destroying our culture. Sodom should be a lesson for us to admit that man in his selfish greed and desire for instant gratification is destroying himself and causing major problems for those with whom they rub shoulders. Just as people of Sodom sought fulfillment through sexual gratification, our culture has become a society that lives for instant gratification. Unfortunately, instant gratification outside God's beautiful plan results in disappointment and regret.

Progressives deliberately misinterpret the story of Sodom and the validity of Biblical truth in this story. They ignore it as if it were outdated and no longer relevant. They embrace the absurd theory of evolution. This is all it is—just a theory that cannot be sustained or supported with truthful facts. If there is no validity to absolute Biblical truth, why does the left feel so threatened? Why do they respond with anger and hate language? What are they afraid of?

When Piers Morgan interviewed Kirk Cameron who calmly and humbly spoke the truth regarding marriage, Piers called Kirk's remarks an opinion that he had no right to impose on others. There was no imposition yet it was obvious that Piers felt threatened and suggested Kirk keep his religion to himself. Why did the liberal media respond with such anger when Phil Robertson of Duck Dynasty quoted the Bible in answer to their question? They are intolerant of our answers, but they expect us to be tolerant of their unnatural and harmful lifestyle.

Here is a question that begs for a reasonable answer. Are human beings actually evolving from reasonable, normal sexuality to an unnatural perverted sexual orientation? If so, did the Creator lie to us because He does not really want what is best for us? Perhaps it was a fluke of evolution that got us into this mess. Believers in evolution have gotten so extreme in their beliefs that they are actually trying to make their system work. When people refuse to accept who they are in relation to God's plan, they take hormones to bring their bodies into conjunction with their minds. Those who call themselves transsexual go a step farther and have surgery to help bring their bodies and their minds into compliance. I have counseled with several transsexuals who have had gender change surgeries. Most of the surgeries have to do with external plumbing.

Speaking of plumbing, our All Wise Creator did a fantastic job of creating male and female with both internal and external plumbing that complements each other perfectly for the purpose of procreation and rec-creation.

I consider myself to be somewhat of a handyman. I have done a few plumbing jobs in my lifetime. I learned that male and female plumbing parts complement each other beautifully. Another good illustration is the function of male and female parts of an extremely valuable mechanism used in seat belts. In addition, I learned quickly that two male or two female parts don't work together. While surgeons have had minimal success with external plumbing changes, internal plumbing changes for the sake of child bearing is impossible.

Some homosexuals may argue that two men can complement each other for pleasure. Having said that, two men or two women cannot bear a child.

Having counseled with those who have had sex change surgery, I can tell you there are enormous ongoing complications. Whatever happened to con-science, commonsense, and logic? It seems to have eluded those who have rejected God's wisdom and principles to live by. It would be a whole lot better for the client, their family, and friends just to seek solutions to the problems in the context of who we are in relation to God's plan. On the other hand, could it just be that sinful man, like Adam and Eve, listen to Satan rather than the Creator?

Back in the 60's, 70's, and 80's society coined a new phrase by which millions of people pattern their lives. "Do your Own Thing!" Reality is they just revived the Old Testament statement, "every man did that which was right in his own sight." The do your own thing expanded to include, "believe your own truth". It is no wonder we are living in an age of sexual confusion. It is time we get honest with ourselves and admit that the ever-changing theory has failed us.

In a letter to the editor, a proponent of sexual expression backhandedly attacked conservative Christians for their stand against same sex unions. He raised the following question—which values should we teach— ignorance, intolerance, discrimination, and hate as acceptable or that we should respect one another and care about other peoples' feelings regardless of our differences? A more honest question should be what makes more sense, believing what the Creator has to say about His plan for sexual fulfillment or believe Afred C. Kinsey's admittedly flawed study about homosexuality as his truth? In Romans 1:25 it says, "They changed the truth of God into a lie and worshipped and served the creature more than the Creator."

Due to the rejection of the Creator, the perfect Designer and Planner for humanity, the moral standards we used to live by have gone awry. Deceit and fraud have infiltrated governments and the business world. Where there was once trust, jealousy and selfishness have bred distrust. As a society, we are living in denial. While I am speaking in generalities, each one of us as individuals, due to our God given conscience, knows where we fall short of the Divinely given principles that bring order instead of chaos when we choose to apply them to our personal lives.

In two hundred fifty years of American history, we have not had the need for numerous ordinances to protect those who have chosen a deviant lifestyle. Having said that, there are laws on the books to protect all citizens equally. We don't need special ordinances to force us to protect minority groups.

We will never solve the problems related to sexual immorality unless we embrace the truth, call it a moral issue, and acknowledge the fact that the Creator designed the beautiful concept of human sexuality.

When people reject the Creator, they are stuck with the conundrum of how we got here. In discussing this issue, some people have a dilemma as to why or how they were born gay or lesbian. In the same conversation, they use the term sexual preference. In doing so, they are contradicting themselves. Isn't this an admission of choice? Albeit wrong choice!

President Obama continued championing his cause for immoral same-sex marriage in his speech to promote gun control. It is not my intent to comment on gun control as this book is about sexual morality. I only mentioned the gun issue because the President continues to exploit every opportunity to promote homosexuality. However, it should be noted that far more lives, marriages, and families are destroyed due to the impact of immoral sexuality on society than by guns.

Supreme Court Justice Antonin Scalia, a principled man of character, passed away February 13, 2016. The following are 2 quotes from Justice Scalia:

"Same-sex union is not announcing a Constitutional right to same-sex marriage"

"Homosexual conduct was a crime for 200 years in every state."

CHAPTER 40
REVEALING THE MYSTERY

Hebrews 13:4 "Marriage is honorable—the bed is undefiled; but fornicators and adulterers God will judge." This text makes it clear that nudity and sexual activity between husband and wife is acceptable and blessed by God. Modesty should be the dress in the presence of all others. Conscience and common sense tell us that modesty is reasonable and logical, yet Hollywood mocks this. Because of the way the liberal media has flaunted sex and nudity, it is almost impossible to view the opposite sex wholesomely. When I grew up in the 40's and 50's we treated girls with respect. Somehow, we just knew that girls were special, and we treated them as such. We treated them like young ladies. We never used vulgar language in their presence. We did not touch girls inappropriately causing them to be aroused. We didn't even hint at having sex with a girlfriend. Carrying books and opening doors for a girlfriend was fun and fulfilling. Just holding hands was special. That does not mean we didn't have hormones. We patiently and longingly looked forward to the day we could share intimacy with a wife on the honeymoon after the commitment stated in the wedding vows.

From personal experience, let me tell you it was a thrill for that which was mysterious to become a reality without guilt. Webster's definition of mysterious: excites curiosity, amazement, and a sudden wave of excitement. To see my new bride in her beautiful wedding dress followed by seeing her nude body for the first time was exciting beyond my expectations. Then to touch her beautiful, delicate body, there is no adjective that could express my thoughts and feelings. This experience helped me understand more clearly Solomon's beautiful descriptive love story in Song of Solomon. Although I am not very musical, and definitely not a songwriter, I find myself periodically putting music to Solomon's words.

When people are sexually intimate before marriage, the excitement, anticipation, and thrill of the wedding and honeymoon are absent. Knowing that God's rules have been violated, leaves both parties with guilt, shame, and fear. The fear of unwanted pregnancy, broken trust, fear of failure early in marriage compounds guilt.

In the Old Testament, the word KNOW is used numerous times. It was not always used in the sense of gaining knowledge. It meant husband and wife coming together in sexual intimacy. In Philippians 3:10 Paul said, "That I may KNOW Him and the power of His resurrection." He was saying I want to KNOW God more intimately. I want to have a closer relationship with Christ. Paul also acknowledged his need for the Holy Spirit's power of the Resurrected Christ. Previously, I made reference to the power and explosion of intimacy when the bride and bridegroom come together in the marriage union. Knowing God and experiencing His power is a necessity for living righteously. Daniel 11:32 says, "The people that KNOW their God shall be strong (powerful) and do exploits." John 14:12 Jesus said, "You will do greater works than I do." This can only be possible through KNOWING God intimately and allowing His Holy Spirit to empower us.

The character of God is revealed in the typology of marriage. God never spoke of a loving same-sex marriage. God never blessed a deviant sexual union. In fact, He condemned homosexuality and pronounced judgment on unrepentant homosexuals. Yes, there are priests and ministers who pronounce blessings on sinful behavior. They will have to answer to God, the Creator of sex. They take Scriptures out of context knowingly and purposefully misinterpret them to defend their reasons for supporting perverted sexual behavior. They exchange truth for a Lie. Roman 1:2 God is Truth and speaks Truth and He does not change.

We attended a graduation service at a state college. The young lady speaking on behalf of the associated students said, "One thing we now know is there can be no absolute truth." This is a contradiction to a statement she made that was printed in the program. She said, "I urge you to always remember why you chose your respective field of study and the sacrifices you endured in order to succeed, enabling you to serve our communities and improve the quality of life and health for all—with compassion, honesty, and integrity."

If there is no absolute truth how do we determine who is honest? Is it any wonder there is so much confusion and turmoil in the minds of our vulnerable students who are trying to find their way. Israel in the Old Testament is a type of the believer in the New Testament. Israel's relationship with God is a type of spiritual marriage, the believer being the Bride, and Christ being the Bridegroom. In Exodus 20:5 in reference to His people Israel, God makes it known that He is a jealous God when He says, "You shall not bow down to any idol or serve them for I, the Lord your God, am a jealous God." Idol worship in the Old Testament is a type of adultery in the New Testament.

The greatest fulfillment in marriage comes solely from focusing on one's spouse, not just from focusing on the sexual experience. Fulfillment comes from bringing pleasure to one's lover in the context of marriage, not from seeking self-pleasure.

Kate and I are now in our mid-seventies. She is just as beautiful to me, both clothed and unclothed, as the day we got married. The excitement has not diminished. She is still desirous to me and for me. She tells me regularly that she loves me more now, and our marriage is stronger than when we first got married.

Marital intimacy is still fulfilling. Candace Cameron, in being interviewed on the Insider TV program, about marriage, her family, and her relationship with God said, "Sex is a very important part of marriage and we shouldn't have to feel shame."

By the way, Kate is typing this manuscript for me. She is embarrassed by my sharing our intimate thoughts. I told her I would give her the opportunity to share her thoughts. The following are her unedited remarks:

By being Ron's typist, I am quite familiar with the thoughts and ideas he is sharing in this book. He is still in training, but I love him anyway. As a nurse and especially the last few years when I worked on the psychiatric unit, I listened to unbelievable stories, heartbreaking ones that made me want to weep. I was reminded daily that as humans we do reap what we sow, not only physically, but also emotionally, mentally, and sexually. What we eat and feed our minds with will come back to haunt us. I have been greatly blessed in my life, my marriage, and as a mother. I prayed for years for a husband who would love God and me! I did find THAT MAN!

I never had to worry about Kate having an affair, and I have never given her a reason to think that I would. I am a jealous husband! I do not want anyone else to share the experience of joy and pleasure that belongs only to us. Thanks Honey for keeping yourself just for me.

In 2 Corinthians 11:2 the Bible says, "I am jealous for you for I have betrothed you to one husband that I may present you a chaste virgin to Christ." Jesus made it very clear that He was a jealous God. Sexual intimacy is a reflection of the Holy Spirit operating between Christ, the Bridegroom, and the people of faith being the bride. The Bridegroom said he would share His glory only with His bride. In other words, He would bring great pleasure to His bride.

I do not want to give the impression that married life was always perfect for us. The following are a few trials we have experienced over the years. Shortly before we got married, I broke my ankle and had complications for several years. Now we are still having complications from the injuries and illnesses listed below: My breaking a leg and shattering it into 30 pieces, injuring both shoulders and tearing a rotator cuff in one; being in an automobile accident where Kate, our daughter, and I suffered from serious injuries. Kate having the most serious injuries had to have her neck fused. Kate battling cancer for 5 years, and our trying to figure out how to pay the medical bills. The aforementioned were major stress factors in our lives. However, we have chosen through our commitment to God and each other to let these trials strengthen our relationship rather than allowing them to destroy it.

I am writing this page on Valentine's Day. I just turned the TV news on; the commentator was telling a love story about a very elderly couple and how their relationship had grown as they got older. Natalie Morales was obviously moved and remarked, "We need more stories like that." This story reminded me of another Valentine story of a few years ago. The couple was celebrating their 80th wedding anniversary.

The gal that was interviewing them was seated with them in their living room. The husband was sitting in his recliner with a newspaper on his lap. The wife was sitting in her rocking chair knitting while being interviewed. The interviewer asked them what the secret was to a long happy marriage. In unison they both said, "Good communication." The interviewer responded by saying, "I have been here for approximately 30 minutes and I have not seen much interaction." The wife turned toward her husband as he said, "There is more than one way to communicate." The way they looked at each other you could actually feel the love they had for each other.

While this couple sat in separate chairs, Kate and I usually sit together in our reclining loveseat. We enjoy sitting next to each other watching TV, reading, and discussing the day's events while holding hands.

We have traveled around the world together. And yes, we are still holding hands wherever we go. Let me tell you a funny story. A few years ago, we were in Israel with our friend, Dave Dolan, who lives in Jerusalem. He was our tour guide. We were walking toward the Temple Mount when we were approached by a man screaming at us. We could not understand him. He continued to scream while pointing at the back of his hand. Dave said, "Just ignore him." We started to walk away. He came after us, screaming louder as he kept pointing to the back of his hand. Dave walked over to him to see if he could find out what was so upsetting.

Eventually, Dave was able to decipher enough of his Arabic language to determine what the problem was. It turned out that Kate and I were violating this sacred place by holding hands.

Recently there has been a considerable amount of news of the happenings in the Ukraine. Watching the news brought back memories of when I was ministering in the Ukraine when it was still under the rule of the former Soviet Union. Even though it was during a time of tension due to the communist control, I had the opportunity to observe a wedding in the Ukraine. In spite of communism and uncertainty, the bride and groom were extremely optimistic about their future together. As it should be, marriage is a new beginning for the bride and groom as they become one as husband and wife united physically, emotionally, socially, and spiritually.

God's plan in Genesis (the first book in the Bible) was to complete Adam by His provision of Eve. In the book of Revelation, the last book of the Bible, God's culmination for man on this earth ends with Christ, the Bridegroom, receiving His bride dressed in white (a symbol of purity). The Bride of Christ is all of the people who have acknowledged and confessed their sins and humbly repented (turned away from their sins).

Earlier I mentioned Abraham and King David. They experienced God's blessing of living eternally in the presence of Christ, the Bridegroom, because they repented. You can, too!

Christ, our Bridegroom, always puts us, His Bride, first. A recent survey by the Pew Research Center shows that 39 percent of the American people feel that the traditional family is obsolete, no longer relevant. They have embraced the philosophy that family can be whatever you want it to be.

In some cultures, marriages are arranged. The future bride and groom do not experience dating that leads to falling in love. I often wonder how these marriages survive versus Western culture marriages.

Recently, Kate and I met a delightful young couple from Bangladesh. While sharing experiences, we learned their marriage was an arranged marriage. In fact, they never met each other until the wedding ceremony was over. Having grown up where this is customary, it did not seem strange to them. Sixteen years later, it is obvious they are still madly in love.

Regardless of why people marry or what kind of ceremony they have, the answer to a good marriage is found in obedience to God. Interestingly enough, God did not tell us to marry the person with whom we fell in love. He told us to love the person we were married to. Years ago, I read a book titled, "Do Yourself a Favor, Love Your Wife." While this book is probably out of print, I would recommend to all men the principles found therein.

Perhaps you could find a copy at a used bookstore.

CHAPTER 41
CONSEQUENCES OF THE UNREPENTANT

There are three distinct situations in the subject matter of this book that I made reference to which cause a Holy God to become irate and pronounce extremely harsh penalties. The first was the abuse of innocent children by pedophilia, and other forms of sex abuse. Jesus said, *"A millstone should be hung around the offender's neck and he should be thrown into the water and drowned."* Secondly, God explained the difference between sexual sin and all other sin when He made it clear, in 1 Corinthians 5:9-10, that unrepentant sexual sinners would have no place in God's kingdom. Thirdly, in Romans, Chapter 1, the penalty for homosexuality would be a two-fold, excessive judgment that God allowed them to bring on themselves and God's pronouncement of death because of their defiance to the Truth and God's plan for their good.

The reason Gods' judgment is so harsh is because people who choose this perverted lifestyle not only practice this deviant behavior, they are doing everything in their power to force their unnatural, unhealthy, abnormal, immoral behavior on the rest of society. In addition, the very nature of homosexuality is an insulting affront to the character and person of a Holy God. As I have tried to convey earlier, God created male and female to share their lives together in the sacred marriage union. That union is a type of the relationship between Christ (the Bridegroom) and the Bride (the people of faith). The Holy Spirit is the unifying factor of which we are overwhelmed with the presence of God.

It has been my goal to tell you the truth about sex according to God's plan. You have read the stories of those who have so graciously agreed to share their experiences. Some were sex offenders and some were sexually abused. In every story, these people would say free sex is not free. There is a very high cost for violating God's plan. In fact, bondage would more accurately describe their experiences. In cases where deviant sexual practices became an addiction, bondage is probably not a strong enough descriptive term. Imprisoned would be more accurate! In Exodus 20, God gave us the Ten Commandments. They were not suggestions! However, one commandment pertains to the content of this book. The commandment is, "Thou shall not commit adultery." Meaning, that we should only have sex with our spouse. Mankind, like Adam and Eve, seems driven to do the very thing that God tells us NOT to do. Interestingly enough, Jesus made only one exception for divorce and remarriage. That was for the innocent party, only when one's spouse commits adultery.

I have spent a considerable amount of time explaining the problems and costs related to sexual immorality. However, I will be spending considerably less time dealing with the solutions to the problems. The TRUTH is not complicated, yet man in his pride and self-centeredness still thinks he can handle things on his own terms. He thinks he can improve on God's plan.

Abram and Sarai were sincere and obviously meant well when they tried to help God out. Deception by Abram when he told Sarai to tell Pharaoh she was his sister caused problems for Pharaoh when he took Sarai to be his wife. This caused distrust between Abram, Sarai, and Pharaoh. Abram, his family and servants had gone to Egypt to find food because of a famine in their country. Because of the deceptive scheme, Pharaoh became angry and told Abram to take his wife and leave.

Abram and Sarai wanted to have children to carry on the family name. When Sarai could not bear children, she came up with a scheme to help God out. She offered her Egyptian servant, Hagar, to Abram. Instead of listening to God, he went along with Sarah's scheme. When Hagar conceived, Sarah got angry and looked on her with contempt. Then Sarah became pregnant and bore Abraham a son. In her anger, she demanded that Abraham should tell Hagar to take her son, Ishmael, and leave. Ishmael grew up in the wilderness and could not get along with anybody. Because of Abraham's disobedience in impregnating Hagar, a barrier came between Isaac and Ishmael, resulting in the early beginnings of terrorism. Isaac and Ishmael's descendants are at odds to this day. Abraham and Sarah's disobedience continues to have a destructive impact all around the world. The cost of terrorism is a tremendous drain on the economy due to the economic demand to fund the CIA and the military. This does not take into consideration the loss of life, limb, psyche, and infrastructure.

Man has been successful in destroying himself and his fellow man. He has failed to live up to the standard that God has set for us in the area of sexuality, because he has rejected the TRUTH. Man in his despair is trying to rewrite history. In his rejection of God, he says the story of Sodom is no longer relevant. Liberals despise accurate history because it reveals the truth and convicts them of their perverted beliefs and practices.

True history always supports the facts. Man may be able to change a few words or phrases, but he can never change the truth. Instead of learning about history, evolutionist and liberal theologians reject the Creator and the story of Sodom. In their bizarre interpretation, they say the story is about hospitality, not sexual immorality. They ignored the facts regarding nations and cultures that have fallen because of immorality (especially homosexuality).

God's Word makes it clear that we have all committed SIN and that we are all deserving of capital punishment. Unfortunately, prideful man thinks he should be the decider of which sexual acts are sin. He argues that customs or traditions should be the deciding factor. In the modern world, we are allowing legislation and the courts to decide right from wrong. However, we are moving rapidly toward every man deciding for himself. Because of this attitude man is not only rewriting history, he is making a valiant attempt at rewriting God's laws and principles. In the end he will fail. Nonetheless, God in His justice has already decided what the rules are and what the penalty will be.

CHAPTER 42
LOVE OVER FEAR

For the past three years, The Human Rights Institute and the Kootenai County Task Force On Human Relations in conjunction with Global Love Day have sponsored, "Choose Love over Fear Day." Tony Stewart, spokesperson for Human rights in North Idaho, attributes Mother Teresa, Martin Luther King Jr., and Mahatma Gandhi, with showing us a path to unconditional love. Mr. Stewart said, "It is not loving to remain silent in the face of hateful or degrading actions against anyone based on their race, nationality, color, origin, gender, age, disability, SEXUAL ORIENTATION, or socio-economic status. True love for humanity does not allow for prejudice, for bigotry, or for discrimination directed toward God's children. It is about action. And true love demands acts of love."

The concept is great. I agree with most of Tony's statements. He acknowledged God as Creator when he referred to God's children. However, in his reference to sexual orientation he included numerous deviant and perverted sexual practices as sexual orientations. God created only TWO sexual orientations, Male and Female. God calls perverted sex an abominable sin. Tony implies that those who reject deviant sex are prejudiced, hateful, and discriminatory bigots.

God had a superior plan as told in the next chapter. He didn't only tell us to love our neighbors, He taught us by example how to love our enemies. His character is revealed in John 4:8 "God is Love" and Proverbs 10:12 "Love covers all sin."

CHAPTER 43
GREATEST LOVE STORY

In the Old Testament, we read prophetic statements made by men of God in regard to the coming and fulfillment of the Story. These prophesies tell us the purpose of the Story, to whom it was written, and give us information about God's character and attributes.

Earlier I mentioned that intimacy was a type of the Holy Spirit. When the bride and groom come together intimately the result is the birth of a child. Likewise, God, our Heavenly Father, impregnated Mary who bore God's son Jesus.

Matthew 1:20 tells us Mary, a virgin, would conceive in her womb a child by the Holy Spirit. Humanly speaking, when a child is born to his parents we refer to it as a blessing. When a child is conceived without the role of a human father, we call it a mystery or a miracle. The birth of Christ has been called the greatest miracle of all time.

Mary was told in advance that the baby would be called Jesus and that He would save His people from their sins. The rest of the Story is all about Jesus, the Savior of the world. This story is comprised of the two most celebrated days in the history of the world, Christmas and Easter. Both days revolve around a miracle: The Birth of Christ and the Resurrection of Christ. Both are necessary for the completion of God's plan. Both are necessary for man's salvation and redemption.

The following are the words of a Christmas song penned by a very close friend of our family, Rev. William Booth-Clibborn, to the tune of "O Sole Mio". I can remember Booth, as we called him, as early as four years of age.

He wrote the song in 1921. Booth left an impression on me that impacts my life and ministry to this day. As I just mentioned, the Love Story brings Christmas and Easter together. Somehow, Rev. Booth-Clibborn understood the significance of two in one. He intended for the song to be a Christmas song, however, over the years it has been sung more at Easter than Christmas.

Down From His Glory
Down from His Glory, Ever living Story
My God and Savior came, and Jesus was His name
Born in a manger, To His own a stranger,
A Man of sorrows, tears and agony

What condescension, Bring us to redemption
That in the dead of night, Not one faint hope in sight
God gracious tender, Laid aside His splendor
Stooping to woo, to win, to save – my soul

Without reluctance, flesh and blood His substance
He took the form of man, revealed the hidden plan
O glorious mystery, sacrifice of Calvary
And now I know He is the Great "I AM"

(Chorus)
O how I love Him, how I adore Him
My breath my sunshine, my all in all
The great Creator became my Savior
And all God's fullness dwelleth in Him

The Love Story is encapsulated in a nutshell in the most quoted verse in the Bible, John 3:16, "God so loved the world that He gave His only begotten Son that whosoever believeth in Him shall not perish but have everlasting life." This is the Story of HOPE! By receiving the Christ of the miraculous birth who is the crucified Christ of the Resurrection, we can be free from the bondage of guilt and the penalty of sin. You say it seems so simple. Compared to the complexity and complications of a sinful life, especially a life of sexual sin, the solution is wonderfully freeing and simple.

Romans 3:23 says, "All have sinned and come short" of God's standard. All means every one of us; from those who have committed a one-night stand of fornication to the millions of people who are addicted to pornography, to those who have committed homosexual acts, to those who have sexually abused a child, to those who have committed the sin of lust, etc. We have ALL sinned. Not one of us is good enough to have a right relationship with God by our own merits.

D.L. Moody said upon seeing the drunk in the gutter, "But for the grace of God, there go I."

Shamyl's Story

I would like to share with you a story that I trust will help you better understand God's purpose and intent for His love story. I first heard this story from my good friend the late Norm Wyman from Australia, approximately 50 years ago. I shared this story from time to time when I was doing high school and college campus ministry in Canada.

This story took place in the part of the world, which is now Afghanistan approximately 200 years ago. There were a number of barbaric tribes that inhabited the mountainous country. Just like today, there were ongoing wars in the region. As the story was told to me, there seemed to be little or no reason for the constant fighting between the various tribes who wanted to control the entire region.

The leader of one of these tribes was Schamyl. He was a strong leader with a brilliant mind when it came to war strategy. The result was this tribe dominated the area for many years. Tradition was that prior to the warriors leaving the home compound to do battle with another tribe, the whole tribe would send the warriors off with a pep rally, during which time they worked themselves into a frenzy. Also, when a battle was won, there would be a huge victory celebration sometimes lasting for several days.

Amongst these warring tribes, there was considerable vicious brutality with much bloodshed and killing. There was raping of the women and sex abuse of children.

While Schamyl was considered to be a great leader, he participated in these atrocities. However, periodically, his conscience bothered him and he felt guilt. Then one day a couple of visitors from another country visited his tribe. Schamyl wanted to know who these people were, and why they came to the camp. He invited them to his tent. They were missionaries. They had a story to tell that could change the lives of the tribe's people so they wouldn't have to live with the guilt of brutalizing people.

Schamyl listened intently and, eventually, he accepted their message and asked God to forgive him. After the missionaries left, Schamyl called a meeting of the whole tribe and told all the tribal members about his acceptance of Jesus. He offered to step down from his position as the chief tribal leader. However, the other tribal leaders said they trusted him to do what was right and insisted he continue to be the tribal leader. He responded by saying, if he were to remain leader, there would have to be a number of changes within the tribe regarding the way they lived their lives. He said they would have to stop lying, cheating, stealing, bribing, abusing and murdering people from neighboring tribes. He followed by saying any violation of these rules would incur punishment by receiving lashes at the whipping post.

The people were receptive and things went well. For several months, there was a new attitude and wonderful harmony in the camp. Then one day the inevitable, one of Shamyl's assistants came to him and told him a tribal member had been caught in the act of bribery.

Immediately Shamyl asked, "Who is it?"

His assistant responded, "I can't tell you."

Shamyl snapped, "You will tell me! That person must be taken immediately to the whipping post and receive one hundred lashes across his back. Now tell me, who was it?"

"I can't tell you," said his assistant.

Shamyl was starting to feel angry as he said, "You tell me!"

The assistant thought, *if I tell him he won't follow through with the punishment anyway so I may as well tell him*. While hesitating to speak, he slowly and quietly said, "Shamyl, it was your own mother."

He was caught off guard and didn't know what to say. He dismissed his assistant. Shamyl stayed in his tent for three days. He did not eat and had trouble sleeping as he tried to determine his course of action. His mind ran in circles as he thought about his mother being tied to the whipping post. It was almost more than he could bear as he visualized her being whipped. He thought, "*I can't let this happen to my mother.*"

Then the thought overwhelmed him—if it were someone else's mother, brother, sister, son, or daughter, they would be tied to the whipping post to receive their punishment. He made the decision to do what was right before all the people.

He called all the people together and told them why he had gone into seclusion. He told them how his mind was in overwhelming turmoil and how he had arrived at his decision to have his mother disciplined. He told the people that this was the most difficult decision he had ever made. Then he pointed to three of the village guards and told them to take his mother outside the camp and tie her to the whipping post. He ordered one of the guards to take the whip and proceed with the whipping. Shamyl stood a distance away. He could not look at his mother. The appointed man with the whip raised his arm (there was total silence). He brought his arm forward, when the whip hit her back, she flinched and so did her son. The guard brought the whip backward, then forward, as it hit its mark it seemed to say, "You can't sin and get away with it."

He brought the whip backward, then forward a third time. It seemed to say even louder, "You can't sin and get away with it." He brought it back the fourth time. Just as he started to move forward, Shamyl yelled out, "Stop it!"

A hush fell over the camp. No one said a word. Some were thinking, "I knew he couldn't do it."

Shamyl walked toward the whipping post and said to the guards, "Untie my mother." There was great silence—then he said, "Tie me to the whipping post. I will take the rest of the beating."

One man came forward and said, "Mr. Shamyl, you can't do that, you are a good man, you didn't do anything wrong." Shamyl responded, "Yes I can, I am the leader, I made the rules, and decided what the penalty should be for bribery, but I didn't say who should take the punishment. Now, tie me to the whipping post."

When the signal was given, the man with the whip proceeded to whip Shamyl. Each time the whip came forward and tore into his flesh, it seemed to say louder, and LOUDER, "YOU CAN'T SIN AND GET AWAY WITH IT!" It didn't only say this to Shamyl, it said this to all who were observing the whipping. It was even saying it to the man with the whip in his hand, but it was screaming louder and louder and louder to Shamyl's mother—*"You can't sin and get away with it."*

For 97 times the whip tore into his flesh. When the beating was finished, they untied Shamyl. His back was bleeding profusely. He slumped forward in a semi-conscious state. His mother ran to him, threw her arms around him and said, "Son, why did you do it?"

With a weakened voice Shamyl said, "Because I love you Mother."

If you saw The Passion of Christ by Mel Gibson and/or The Son of God, hopefully, you will understand about God's great love for us when He sent His son Jesus to die on the cross to pay the penalty for our sins. I trust the illustration in the story about Shamyl will help you understand more clearly how much God hates sin, but also how much He loves you!

In the New Testament, Jesus gave us a new commandment. In the new law, we are commanded to love God with our whole being and our neighbor as ourself. Love then becomes the solution to the problem. God told us in 1 John that if we love Him, we will obey Him. If we truly love God and our neighbor, we will view humanity from God's perspective. We will not have a desire to harm those we love.

Also, God commands husbands to love their wives, Ephesians 5:22-33. He tells wives to love their husbands and their children, Titus 2:4.

In spite of man's rebellion, God is still a God of love. He continues to show His love by His provision and His protection. Many years ago the title of a song that was rated number one, was, "What the World Needs Now is Love". The composer was right, but man in his humanness is not capable of fully loving God or man. In First Corinthians 13 love is beautifully defined. The Bible tells us without love we have nothing.

Rusty Goodman wrote the words to this song, which attempts to describe God's great love:

"If you could own all the world and its money,
build castles tall enough to reach the sky above,
If you could know everything there was to know
about life's game, yet you've known nothing
until you've known God and His love. Until you've
known the loving hand that reaches down to a fallen man
and lifts him up from out of sin where he has trod
Until you've known just how it feels to know that God
Is really real, then you've known nothing until you've known
God and His love."

We also read in God's word that "God is Love". I recently heard a minister make this statement, "God's love is big enough to accept the greatest repentant sinner, but small enough to exclude the most minute unrepentant sinner." This love story was conceived in the mind of the Creator in history past. History means "His Story". (God's Story).

It has been said that love demands an object. God is pleading for you to be the object of His love. In 1 Corinthians 13:8 the Bible says, *"Love never fails."* Frederick Lehman in the hymn he wrote, "The Love of God" gives us a glimpse of how great God's love is:

"The love of God is greater far than tongue or pen
Can ever tell, it goes beyond the highest star
And reaches to the lowest hell.
Could we with ink the ocean fill, and were the skies

Of parchment made, were every stalk on earth a quill.
And every man a scribe by trade
To write the love of God above would drain the ocean
dry, nor could the scroll contain the whole, though
Stretched from sky to sky."

Recently, Kate and I went to see Son of God. It was one of the best portrayals I have ever seen of the life, death, and resurrection of Jesus Christ. The reminder of His sacrifice for me in paying the penalty for my sin, made me appreciate God's love more than ever. Just as those who hated Jesus and detested the cross over 2000 years ago, some of you who are reading this book continue to reject Christ and the Cross. I beg you to accept His love and embrace the Cross. Romans 5:8 "God commended His love to us, in that while we were yet sinners, Christ died for us."

We must confess our sins and ask God for forgiveness (acknowledge that we are not worthy). The Bible describes our sin as filthy rags. We are deserving of God's judgment. Romans 6:23, "The wages of sin is death" (eternal separation from God). "But the gift of God is eternal life through Jesus Christ our Lord." The greatest love story is about Jesus Christ. In this text, God is offering His Son Jesus as His love gift to us to pay our death penalty. All that is necessary for us is by faith to receive God's love gift followed by repentance. Repent means to turn around and go the other direction. In other words, turn away from and stop committing sinful acts. Jesus said to the woman who was caught in the act of adultery, "Go and sin no more," meaning run as far and as fast as you can from the possibility of entrapment.

God's warnings to us are because He loves us. Our response to a loving God should be a love for Jesus because of all He has done for us, by taking upon Himself our sins when He went to the cross. He said, "If you love Me, you will obey Me." When we obey Him, we benefit, our families benefit, and society benefits. Psalm 103:12, "As far as the East is from the West so far has He removed our transgressions from us." Jeremiah 31:34, "I will forgive their iniquity, and I will remember their sin no more." *Micah 7:19,* "He will have compassion upon us; He will subdue our iniquities; and Thou wilt cast all their sins into the depths of the sea."

God's word is clear, if we are truly repentant He will remove our sins as far as the East is from the West, He will bury them in the bottom of the deepest sea, (and my favorite part) HE WILL FORGET ALL ABOUT THEM. That should be incentive enough to turn your life over to God and live a righteous life, (righteous meaning right living). Proverbs 14:34, "Righteousness exalteth a nation but sin is a reproach to any people."

God's plan for sexuality, when practiced in our lives, brings blessings. When we operate outside God's beautiful plan, our sexuality becomes a burden. I trust I have given you enough information along with the sampling of testimonies to help you more clearly understand how devastatingly destructive immorality can be to our personal and family lives as well as our culture and society. I hope that in the writing of this treatise I have made it clear that my intent is not to condemn but to share truth. Jesus said, "I am the Way, the TRUTH, and the Life," John 14:6.

"The TRUTH will set you free," John 8:32. "Love rejoices when truth wins out," 1 Corinthians 13:6.

Do yourself a favor, seek TRUTH! Experience LOVE!

CHAPTER 44
POST SCRIPT—HOPE

I was privileged to play a role by my giving input in the wording of the Marriage Amendment Bill and by my testimony in the State Affairs Committee.

My good friend, Mike Duff, and I held the kickoff rally for the statewide petition drive at the Reach America Headquarters in Coeur d' Alene. The purpose of the petition drive was to put pressure on the Legislators to place the Marriage Amendment of one man and one woman on the ballot. The referendum passed and the Amendment was entered into the Idaho State Constitution. However, supporters of political correctness and same-sex marriage continue to cause major divisions among the citizenry. Brazen city council members in several cities arrogantly snubbed the majority of the people in favor of same-sex unions by overriding the Idaho Constitution.

It was a sad day when the court overrode the majority of the people and the State Constitution.

Locally in my home town, the owners of a wedding chapel, called the Hitching Post refused to perform same-sex marriage ceremonies. This case is presently before the courts. To help you better understand the circumstances regarding the Hitching Post, Coeur d'Alene is widely known as the wedding capitol of the Northwest.

Homosexual activists are pressuring city councils and school boards to pass ordinances that will change policies to give special rights to gays and lesbians.

At the time of writing this book, the controversy over natural marriage versus unnatural same-sex marriage was before the Supreme Court of the United States.

Yesterday, I completed this manuscript, or so I thought. I delivered the rough copy for editing. Then today's headline in the Coeur d'Alene Press read....

"2014 A Big Year For Idaho"
GAY MARRIAGE AMONG STATE'S TOP NEWS

The article said four lesbian couples sued to overturn the State's ban on gay marriage. Most Idahoans thought that this could never happen in Idaho! I'm sure that many of you who have read this book are dealing with similar situations in your communities and states

A week later after submitting this manuscript to the publisher, five members of the Supreme Court of the United States overstepped their bounds by acting as if they were the elected members of the Congress. These five members proved to be spineless by violating their own consciences.

On the same day the court ruled in favor of same-sex marriage, the inhabitants of the White House (the people's house) blatantly and arrogantly lit the White House in the colors of the rainbow in celebration of the legality of a perverted sexual lifestyle.

While homosexuals are celebrating as if they have won a major victory, the citizens of Ireland were dancing in the streets after having passed a same-sex law with 62 percent of the vote. However, let me say loud and clear, you cannot mock God and remain victorious. God's Word states clearly that He will judge those who reject His principles and His laws including His beautiful plan for sexuality. Regardless of how the various courts rule in the future the Supreme Judge of the universe will make the final ruling.

My friend, Idaho's Governor, Butch Otter, along with Idaho's Attorney General, Lawrence Wasden, challenged the Ninth District Appellate Court to take a stand in favor of traditional marriage. Gov. Otter requested the members of the United States Supreme Court to support traditional marriage even though members of the Supreme Court overruled the will of the people.

Gov. Butch Otter, in his victory speech upon being re-elected, vowed that he would continue the fight for the Marriage Amendment in the Idaho Constitution even if he has to take it all the way to the Supreme Court. I am asking you to join me in thanking Gov. Otter for not wavering on this most important and sacred issue. Our support for Gov. Otter and Attorney General Wasden is an encouragement to them to continue the fight for traditional marriage.

Because of my involvement, I have a continued interest in this issue. I WILL continue to advocate for morality, truth, and justice. Please join me in the support of the truth. Truth is not always popular. But TRUTH MATTERS and TRUTH always wins!

Second Peter, chapter 5, makes it clear that mankind is WILLINGLY ignorant of God's judgment on those who mock His truth. The emphasis is put on the word WILLINGLY. Conversely, II Peter 3:9 says, "God is not WILLING that any should perish, but that all should come to repentance."

YES THERE IS HOPE!

CHAPTER 45
PARADIGM SHIFT

Recently I attended a seminar. One of the forum topics had to do with a paradigm shift. In the early 60's we began to see and experience a shift when Bible reading and prayer were removed from the public schools. It was about that time that free sex was promoted and became a divisive, destructive factor in the lives of our young people. The question has been asked over and over again, "Why are so many people experimenting with and practicing deviant, perverted sex?" The answer is man has chosen to reject God, the Creator. This has resulted in man having a huge void in his life. In the process of trying to fill that void, he fills it with destructive thoughts and behaviors.

The only way we can expect to experience a new genuine, positive life-changing paradigm shift is to turn from a life of instant gratification, to a life of acting responsibly with God's wonderful gift of sexuality.

It is time we experience a paradigm shift. This time if we want to save this great country, we will need a shift toward the direction of, once again, acknowledging God, our Creator, as did our Founding Fathers. The rule of law based on Biblical morality, the Declaration of Independence, and the United States Constitution must be the foundation of the new paradigm shift.

Throughout the Bible there are numerous references regarding the importance of speaking the truth. However, the same God who hates sin and judges the sinner is also a God of love. He validated His love for us by sending His Son, as ascertained in the greatest love story ever told, to pay the penalty for our sin.

I trust that by my exposing the lies and explaining the truth you will gain a better understanding of God's beautiful creation of man's sexuality and God's desired intimacy with us. Also, I trust that the testimonies of those people who have shared their stories will be an encouragement. They come from various backgrounds. A couple of them are well-known prominent citizens in their communities. All of them have experienced a changed life by surrendering their will by placing their trust in Jesus Christ. YOU CAN TOO!

It is my desire that you experience FREEDOM (freedom from sin, the consequences and judgment for sin, freedom from fear of consequences, freedom from the bondage of sexual addictions—-guilt, depression, anxiety, and freedom from a captive mind, body, and soul). In Ephesians, we read about speaking the truth in love. It has been my desire as I penned the pages in this book to convey an attitude of love while speaking the truth. I am sure there are some things that I have written that may have made you feel uncomfortable. You may have chosen to reject some of God's truths. However, in Galatians 4:16, along with the Apostle Paul, I too ask, "Am I become your enemy because I tell you the truth?"

Regardless of your response, I must continue to speak and write the truth because it is the truth that sets us free from the bondage of sin (including the shackles of sexual immorality). I suggest you review the Greatest Love Story, embrace its principles, celebrate and enjoy the Christ of Christmas and Easter. Be assured the price was paid for all our sins including sexual immorality.

The last chapter of God's word has been written; however, the last chapter of this book will probably not be written until sometime in the future. Please join me as we work together in writing the last chapter by restoring God's beautiful plan for marriage and sexuality. Also it is my desire for you that you experience an eternal intimacy with the Creator.

In 2nd Chronicles 7:14 says, "If My people which are called by My name will humble themselves and pray, and seek my face, and turn from their wicked ways then will I hear from heaven and will heal their land."

This is the kind of paradigm shift that will change our lives for eternity.

In conclusion, let me repeat one more time John 8:32, "The Truth will set you free." John 14:6 Jesus said, "I am the way, the Truth, and the life."

SEX

BADDEST SIN?

OR

GOODEST PLEASURE?

The answer to both questions is YES. Let me explain how I arrived at my answer, and how I chose the title for this book. In the book of Genesis after each of the five days of creation, God said, "It was good." On the sixth day after He created Adam and Eve, He said, "It was VERY GOOD!" The opposite of good is bad or evil. Goodest comes from good and baddest comes from bad.

Adam and Eve disobeyed God. Since then all humanity has fallen into their footsteps. In so doing, we have made a real mess of things, especially in the area of sexuality. However, it was God's plan that sex would be pleasurable and good. God has given us a choice, we can obey Him and enjoy sex to its fullest or we can reject God's plan and do it our way, practice evil and be unfulfilled.

Please Choose God's Way!

I cannot emphasize enough that God, the Creator, had our best interest at heart when He designed male and female to complement each other in marriage. I trust you will have a better understanding of God's plan for sexuality for both procreation and rec-creation.

Sex Can Be the Goodest Pleasure!

You can contact Ron Vieselmeyer for further help in finding forgiveness and freedom as described in the text.

Help Center Counseling Services
A Ministry of Reach America Inc.
1234 W. Appleway, Coeur d'Alene, Idaho 83814, **208-765-2407**